THE LIBRARY
ST. MARY'S COLLEGE OF MARYLAND
ST. MARY'S CITY, MARYLAND 20686

Eugenio Montale

Twayne's World Authors Series
Italian Literature

Anthony Oldcorn, Editor
Brown University

TWAS 778

EUGENIO MONTALE
(1896–1981)
Photograph by Anna Maria Papi

Eugenio Montale

By Jared Becker

Columbia University

Twayne Publishers • *Boston*

Eugenio Montale

Jared Becker

Copyright © 1986 by G.K. Hall & Co.
All Rights Reserved
Published by Twayne Publishers
A Division of G.K. Hall & Co.
70 Lincoln Street
Boston, Massachusetts 02111

Copyediting supervised by Lewis DeSimone
Book production by Elizabeth Todesco
Book design by Barbara Anderson

Typeset in 11 pt. Garamond
by Modern Graphics, Inc., Weymouth, Massachusetts

Printed on permanent/durable acid-free paper
and bound in the United States of America

Library of Congress Cataloging-in-Publication Data

Becker, Jared.
　Eugenio Montale.

　(Twayne's world authors series; TWAS 778.
Italian literature)
　Bibliography: p. 150
　Includes index.
　1. Montale, Eugenio, 1896–　　—Criticism and
interpretation.　I. Title.　II. Series: Twayne's world authors series; TWAS
778.　III. Series: Twayne's world authors series. Italian literature.
PQ4829.O565Z5684　1986　　851'.912　　86–225
ISBN 0-8057-6633-2

Contents

About the Author
Preface
Acknowledgments
Chronology

> Chapter One
> Biography of a Skeptic   1
>
> Chapter Two
> *Ossi di seppia*   20
>
> Chapter Three
> *Le occasioni*   52
>
> Chapter Four
> *La bufera e altro*   86
>
> Chapter Five
> *Satura* and Afterward   117
>
> Chapter Six
> Conclusion   137

Notes and References   141
Selected Bibliography   150
Index   153

About the Author

As an undergraduate, Jared Becker attended Cornell University, where he studied Classics. He received a Ph.D. in Italian literature at Columbia University, and currently teaches there.

Preface

The version of Eugenio Montale offered in these pages is in a number of ways a departure, particularly for English-speaking readers. Montale has had many appreciators in this language he was so fond of, from T. S. Eliot to Robert Lowell, and by now the English-language translations and critical studies devoted to him occupy a full shelf. Nevertheless, he has not been perfectly understood, partly because he was reticent about certain aspects of his work, and partly because the literary and political terrain from which he grew is complex and still lacks complete definition.

In the wake of his Nobel Prize in 1975, and then again following his death in 1981, new information, new analyses, and new editions of Montale's work have appeared. It seems a propitious moment to try to piece together, however provisionally, the partial and often conflicting definitions of this difficult author. One must reconcile, or at least juxtapose, the political poet and the love poet, the landscape poet and the metaphysical poet, the lyrical poet and the satirical poet, the religious poet and the anticlerical poet, the prosaic poet and the musical poet. . . . As even this summary list of paradoxes and antitheses suggests, Montale is not an easy subject to categorize.

This book contains new ideas about the anti-Fascist themes in Montale's poetry, about the female figures that appear so vividly and play such peculiar roles in his verse, about the writer's relationship to literary currents such as "hermeticism" and "decadence," as well as his connection to the literary and cultural critic Benedetto Croce. As one would expect, given the attention Montale has received, none of these topics is completely untouched territory. And the many debts this study owes to its predecessors will be evident, even if the conclusions frequently diverge from those offered in the past. Naturally, given the limitations of space and the biases of the author, this book will not encompass all aspects of the poet's work. But I am confident that Montale will not lack future commentators to widen our understanding of a poetry that stands with ease beside the best modernist writing of the century.

EUGENIO MONTALE

   For criticisms of some of this work when it was a dissertation, I thank Leon Roudiez, Edward Said, and John Nelson. In addition to supplying valuable general suggestions on Montale, Olga Ragusa expertly edited an article of mine on the poet's antifascism, portions of which are included here. My gratitude also goes to Anthony Oldcorn, my Twayne field editor. Last but hardly least, I thank Luciano Rebay for many years of encouragement and much good advice on Montale.

Jared Becker

Columbia University

Acknowledgments

Grateful acknowledgment is given to *Italica* for permission to use portions of my article " 'What We Are *Not*': Montale's Anti-Fascism Revisited" 60, no. 4 (Winter 1983): 331–39; acknowledgment is also given to *Italian Quarterly* for permission to use parts of my forthcoming article "Decadence Defended: Montale's 'Botta e risposta I.' "

Montale's poetry, *Ossi di seppia, Le occasioni, La bufera e altro, Satura, Diario del '71 e del '72, Quaderno di quattro anni,* and *Altri versi,* is copyrighted 1948, 1949, 1957, 1971, 1973, 1977, and 1981 by Arnoldo Mondadori Editore. Permission to quote from the Italian version of Montale's verse is given by New Directions Publishing Corporation, publisher of Montale's *Selected Poems* (1965), *New Poems* (1976), and *It Depends: A Poet's Notebook* (1980).

Quotations of Montale's poetry in this book are from Eugenio Montale, *Tutte le poesie* (Milano: Mondadori, 1977), abbreviated TLP. Translations are my own.

Chronology

1896   Eugenio Montale born in Genoa.

1905   Family villa at Monterosso constructed. Household members and acquaintances, among them a girl called "Arletta," will furnish inspiration for many characters appearing in poet's work.

1916   After death of Sivori, Montale gives up ambition to become opera singer. Writes first version of "Meriggiare pallido e assorto," later included in *Ossi di seppia*.

1917–1919   Called to serve in World War I, Montale attends Officers Training School. Serves on Austrian front. Demobilized in 1919 and returns to Genoa.

1925   Publishes statement of poetics, "Style and Tradition," in Piero Gobetti's magazine *Il Baretti*. Gobetti issues Montale's first collection of verse, *Ossi di seppia*. Poet signs Croce's manifesto countering declaration published by congress of Fascist intellectuals. First of Montale's many appreciations of novelist Italo Svevo.

1927   Moves to Florence to work for Bemporad Publishing House. Contributes frequently to literary journals.

1929   Becomes director of the Vieusseux Library in Florence.

1931   Publishes *La casa dei doganieri*. Meets future wife, Drusilla Tanzi ("Mosca"), and will shortly encounter Irma Brandeis ("Clizia"), an American Dante scholar.

1938   Removed from post at Vieusseux because he is not member of Fascist Party.

1939   Publishes *Le occasioni*, collection of verse incorporating *La casa dei doganieri*, and many Clizia poems.

1943   Gianfranco Contini, critic and confidant of Montale, takes manuscript of "Finisterre" to Switzerland for publication. Epigraph of these pieces is thinly veiled condemnation of Fascist regime.

1945	At close of war, Montale joins Action Party. Poet is intensely occupied with political and cultural polemics.
1948	Becomes full-time contributor to *Corriere della sera*, most authoritative daily paper in Italy. Resides in Milan, but travels frequently as a journalist, especially in Western Europe. Late 1940s are marked by poems to the fox-woman ("Volpe"), a young Italian poetess.
1956	First editions of *La bufera e altro*, incorporating "Finisterre," and *La farfalla di Dinard*, a set of stories and sketches.
1963	Drusilla Tanzi, poet's life-long companion, dies. They had been married shortly before her death.
1971	*Satura*, Montale's fourth major collection of poetry, includes pieces about Mosca. Other verse, in much the same vein as *Satura*, will appear during the poet's final years.
1975	Nobel Prize for Literature.
1980	Contini, dean of Italian philologists and literary critics, publishes critical edition of Montale's verse—an unprecedented event for a living author.
1981	Dies in Milan.

Chapter One
Biography of a Skeptic

Early Years

Eugenio Montale was born in 1896 in Genoa, where his father was a prosperous businessman, the owner of a company that imported chemicals. Since two of his brothers were to join the family firm, while a third would take employment in a bank, one might have predicted a career in business for this youngest son as well. But, as Montale explained many years later in a semifictional account, there was a tradition in well-to-do families of the day, according to which the last son—especially if sickly—could be exempted from the normal middle-class expectations and allowed to devote himself to artistic pursuits. Thus Eugenio was to arrive at the age of thirty without any settled occupation in life. And in the meantime he would cultivate more than one art, perhaps not too differently from the stereotypical turn-of-the-century dandy, except that his vocation as a poet was eventually to become unmistakable.[1]

For a while the young Montale was intent on mastering bel canto and to this end studied with the local maestro Ernesto Sivori, who trained him for such parts as Valentino in Gounod's *Faust* and Alfonso in Donizetti's *La favorita*. The sudden death of Sivori in 1916 put an end to Montale's professional aspirations as a baritone, though his passion for music continued. In fact, the poet once described his verse as springing from an essentially musical impulse[2] (though he also distrusted the "pure poetry," or purely musical verse, which was to become an object of controversy in Italian letters during the 1930s. Some of his first poems, for example, were written in an attempt to imitate Debussy, and still other works from his first season bear such musical titles as "Falsetto" and "Corno inglese" ("English Horn"). A loving evocation of the names of opera characters may be found in a piece of 1929, "Keepsake"—though probably the culmination of Montale's musical career came with his appointment in the 1950s as music critic for the noted Milanese daily *Il Corriere d'Informazione*. In this period his assiduousness in attending opening night performances at La Scala was legendary.

His health judged precarious, Montale was not permitted to finish the technical school in which he was enrolled at Genoa. Nor did he attend the university, though by his own testimony he was a bookworm as an adolescent and taught himself to read French, Spanish, and English. Poetry and philosophy figured in his private studies. He read the French symbolist poets, puzzled through sonnets of Keats, absorbed Cervantes—yet also grappled with the works of Bergson and Boutroux, Gentile and Croce, the philosophers most in vogue at that time in France and Italy. The label "metaphysical" was soon pinned to Montale's early poetry, and his intellectual background does justify reading his verse with an eye to its connections with, for example, Croce's aesthetic theories.

Books were not the young Montale's only fascination. Collected in his memory and much later decanted in the form of short stories are his encounters with an array of eccentric characters. To begin with, there was Sivori, who must have seemed exotic enough with his medals from the Czar and other memorabilia of a peripatetic career. Or a character named Rebillo, who scandalized Genoa's tradition-minded concertgoers with bizarre musical compositions for player piano—works that sounded like sheer noise to audiences that could appreciate nothing more advanced than Wagner. Or the cousin of Montale's father, Lorenzo, who cultivated a garden of cactuses, and knew precisely when each plant in his collection would bloom.[3] Many of these eccentrics, or others observed later in life, find a place in Montale's poetry and prose. And the poet, with his passion for bel canto and later his fancy for painting, probably would not regret being counted among the company of dilettantes. The significance of these odd characters with their strange vocations is that they come to represent for Montale an ideal of individualism and personal freedom which he sets in contrast to the mass movements of his day. And those early years of the century, when the dandy and the dilettante flourished, will constitute in retrospect a sort of Golden Age for him.

In 1905, Montale's father constructed a summer retreat, a villa at Monterosso, on the Ligurian shore south of Genoa. Here the youngest son was to spend his summers for the next twenty-some years. From this severe but beautiful coastal landscape the poet drew the backdrop for his first collection of verse, *Ossi di seppia* (*Bones of the Cuttlefish).* The first poem recognizably in the spirit of the book, "Meriggiare pallido e assorto" ("To spend the noontide, pale and absorbed"), was composed in 1916. It speaks of the noon hour in a sun-baked orchard by the sea, and reports minutely on the comings and goings of ants, and on the harsh music produced by chirping blackbirds, slithering snakes, and whirring cicadas. But the piece does not content itself with mere description. It ends, in a maneuver characteristic of Montale's early poetry, by evoking the narrator's "sad amazement" at seeing all the trials of life summed up, as it were, by a walk beside a garden wall forbiddingly surmounted by shards of broken glass. The landscape is material for the poet, but not an end in itself. From the start he is conscious that description alone, however powerful, cannot suffice.

In 1917 Montale was called to serve in World War I. He attended an officer's training school, where he met others his age with literary interests, among them Sergio Solmi, who was to become a life-long friend and appreciator. Given his commission, the young Montale was assigned to a mountainous section of the Austrian front, northeast of Venice, where a brutal trench warfare was being fought. Very little of his wartime experiences were to sift into Montale's writing. Unlike Giuseppe Ungaretti, perhaps his nearest rival for the title of most influential Italian poet of this century, Montale did not find in the circumstances of war any inspiration for an outpouring of poetry. In pieces such as "Veglia" ("Watch") Ungaretti can describe with a mixture of delirium and exaltation the way in which the horror of the trenches heightens his sense of being alive: beside a dead companion, he writes love letters and feels more "attached to life" than ever before.[4] Montale's biographer records just a few wartime recollections from the poet, including the gruesome and pathetic scene when an Italian soldier was executed by firing squad for pilfering. In *Ossi di seppia* there is a poem about Valmorbia, the outpost where the poet had his command. The piece speaks of the sound of a nearby stream, the foxes that haunted the area, the nights that seemed endlessly lit and sleepless. No passion or excitement fills Montale's version of combat.

World War I, especially in Italy, provides a litmus test for the avant-garde, a way of separating into two distinct groups those who entertained a modernist approach to art. Some, most notably the Futurists, gloried in the battle and its destruction. Everything that undid the traditional order appeared to them automatically worthy of praise. They believed in the virtue of actively destroying, and were glad to see the world in fragments. The other faction—to which Montale clearly belongs—acknowledged the death of the old order, but felt more remorse and disorientation than rejoicing at its collapse. The war cannot be in any way an occasion for celebration in Montale's eyes, and it is no surprise that his postwar visions of disintegration are drawn with somber, not joyful, colors.[5]

Primary Influences

D'Annunzio. Montale was demobilized in 1919 and returned to Genoa. At this point his literary activity intensified, and the next four years yielded most of the poetry that would form *Ossi di seppia.* But in the tumultuous postwar period in Italy, literature was inevitably caught up with politics. As the poet's biographer reports, the young Montale had no sooner begun to circulate in literary society than he was obliged to choose between a café frequented by the partisans of Gabriele D'Annunzio and another establishment more hospitable to the detractors of the renowned poet. D'Annunzio (1863–1938) was among those who had been more thrilled than appalled by the war. As a flying ace he had undertaken daring missions, during one of which he lost an eye; in his poetry figure such items as an ode to a torpedo boat. An ardent nationalist, the soldier-poet was so infuriated by the terms Italy received at Versailles that he personally organized an expedition to conquer Fiume, a city on the Dalmatian coast with a large Italian population, which had been assigned by treaty to the Yugoslavs. Wildly popular for his exploits, D'Annunzio was much admired by Mussolini, and temporarily at least the aims of the two seemed to coincide.

D'Annunzio was not just a military man who dabbled in literature. In Italy he was the most celebrated writer of his day, even if the Nobel Prize of 1906 had gone to the august republican bard Giosuè Carducci (1835–1907), while Giovanni Pascoli (1855–1912), a poet with roots in the countryside of Romagna, also attracted a following. It was D'Annunzio's lyrical voice, finally, that was held to be incomparably musical, even as his novels, dramas, and reportage enjoyed the widest audience. Furthermore, he had a tremendous talent for self-promotion. Just at the dawning of the age of mass media, he intuitively grasped the possibilities for creating a public image and manipulating the multitude to the tune of his whims. At first it was a series of love affairs with such leading ladies as Eleonora Duse that entranced D'Annunzio's audience; later his public was galvanized by his military and political adventures. As early as 1900 in his novel *Il fuoco (The Fire)*, the writer had laid out a blueprint for the artist or intellectual bent on commanding a vast following. The D'Annunzian alter ego in that book mesmerizes a throng with his nationalistic oratory, eliciting from the audience exactly the responses he chooses, just as—to adopt D'Annunzio's metaphor—a virtuoso summons up precisely the music he desires from his instrument. Eventually this scenario was translated into potent reality, for D'Annunzio's little coup d'état on the Dalmatian coast, though ultimately checked by the Italian government, did leave the poet with a formidable following in his country—a constituency that the nascent Fascist movement would seek to appropriate.[6]

Montale chose to frequent the café where the anti-D'Annunzians gathered. Nor is it surprising, considering the enormous influence of the older poet, that Montale should have spent so much energy resisting the example of his predecessor. Indeed his first major essay, "Style and Tradition," published in 1925, was adamant in its refusal of the kind of politicized art that D'Annunzio above all others had propagated. The hallmark of the times, Montale complained, seemed to be a culture designed for immediate consumption—and with this comment he was criticizing that manipulation of the public that D'Annunzio practiced with consummate skill. Montale specifically refuses the older poet's pretensions to the status of "Superman," which, in D'Annunzio's interpretation of the Nietzschean notion, meant shaping a malleable audience to his will. Instead of this version of the artist's vocation, Montale espouses a craft humbly exercised, and an art that will so little raise its voice as to pass practically unnoticed, or even seem "useless" to the public. According to "Style and Tradition," poetry's involvement with politics can only be pernicious, and instead of following D'Annunzio's example the artist ought to maintain a more circumspect relationship with the audience.[7]

On several occasions Montale also comes to grips with D'Annunzio just as a literary influence, so ponderous as to require exorcism if the successor-poets are to develop their own personalities. In the same way that the spirit of Victor Hugo had to be disposed of so that a talent like Baudelaire's could rise, so D'Annunzio, in an analogy that Montale once proposed, constituted an oppressive weight for writers who came after him—simply because his verse had so completely captured the public imagination and had appeared to establish definitively what a poetic voice should be.[8]

The consensus is that *Ossi di seppia* bears numerous signs of Montale's struggle with D'Annunzian influence. As far as politics go, the younger poet certainly dissents from his predecessor's line. Quite explicitly, the lyrical speaker of *Ossi di seppia* rejects the role of the writer whose words are intended to lead people in this direction or that. Furthermore, Montale's very language in his first collection signifies a break with D'Annunzio. In antithesis to the incredibly mellifluous music and grandiose tones of his predecessor, the poet of *Ossi di seppia* frequently adopts grating sounds and harsh rhymes (a technique he learned from Dante, directly and through certain poems of Pascoli), and abandons noble registers for the colloquial. Moreover, Montale's first book shies away from images of a burgeoning, vital nature that dominate D'Annunzio's most famous poetry. The younger writer's impulses sometimes lead him to celebrate nature with a certain ebullience, but he distrusts these tendencies in himself, and more often the landscape he portrays is barren and melancholy, not at all exuberant.[9]

Gobetti. *Ossi di seppia* was published in 1925 by Piero Gobetti, a remarkable man who, though several years younger than Montale, had already made his mark on Italian letters and politics. Gobetti was a one man publishing house, and since the age of seventeen had edited periodicals and books, attracting contributions from the most illustrious names in Italian culture, including the eminent critic Benedetto Croce, the political and economic theorist Luigi Einaudi, and the gadfly intellectual journalist Giuseppe Prezzolini. For four years he published *Rivoluzione liberale (The Liberal Revolution)*, a journal which often did battle with the Fascists, by then installed in Rome and intent on consolidating their power with any means. By personal order of Mussolini, Gobetti was physically harassed and his magazine frequently censored. In 1925, it was finally suppressed completely. But Gobetti in the meantime had laid plans for another review, *Il Baretti,* which began to appear at the end of 1925. Although primarily dedicated to cultural affairs, *Il Baretti* did not really constitute a retreat from politics; it was named after an eighteenth-century man of letters who, having sojourned in places he found enlightened (e.g., England), returned to his native Italy to chastise the torpid, backward peninsula. Gobetti could not direct this new journal for long. Constrained by the violent treatment he received from Fascist shock troops, the editor departed for exile in France. (The story goes that Montale saw him off at the train station.) In 1926 he died in Paris, presumably from the aftereffects of the Fascist beatings.

Gobetti published not only *Ossi di seppia* but also "Style and Tradition," which appeared in *Il Baretti*. One might naturally inquire what affinities—literary and political—linked the publisher and the poet; certainly Montale never failed to speak of Gobetti with profound respect, as, for example, when he commemorated the fiftieth anniversary of the editor's death in an article for the *Corriere della sera*. It is evident, first of all, that the two shared an antipathy for D'Annunzio, who was for Gobetti the bane of Italy and whose disciples were the principal proponents of Fascism. Unlike Montale, however, the publisher did not respond to D'Annunzio the political poet by advocating a general disengagement of art from current affairs. Gobetti was committed to promoting an alliance between the liberal intelligentsia and the left wing of the working class. (This is the concept behind the title *Rivoluzione liberale*.) He violently attacked those like Prezzolini who surrendered their role as political conscience and in the face of Fascism's ever-increasing control of the nation's life, simply withdrew like monks retiring to a convent to wait out another Dark Age. For Gobetti, culture could only be *engagé*—after all, he inaugurated even the ostensibly literary review *Il Baretti* with a denunciation of the barbarous Fascist regime and its D'Annunzian courtiers.

One part of Gobetti's anti-Fascism with which Montale surely empathized was the editor's championing of a European outlook rather than a narrowly nationalistic one. In terms of literature, this meant an openness to contemporary French and German writers such as Proust, Valéry, and Brecht, all discussed in *Il Baretti*. Montale admired these cosmopolitan interests, and especially Gobetti's sympathy for modernism. In 1926, Montale would favorably review James Joyce's *Dubliners,* and in the previous year he had given the first serious critical attention to Joyce's friend Italo Svevo, a Triestine writer whose novels had been all but ignored in his native Italy but who was soon to be discovered by Parisian literary circles. As Fascism strengthened its hold on Italy, nationalistic cultural movements emerged, and critics were discouraged from paying homage to foreign art and literature. But Montale, like Gobetti, refused this direction; throughout the twenty years of the regime the poet remained receptive to cosmopolitan influences, writing pieces on French, English, and American authors.[10]

Montale also found congenial Gobetti's hope that the liberal intelligentsia would have a special role in forging a better Italy—though the poet did not share the editor's equal appreciation for the importance of a radicalized proletariat. In fact, in an essay that appeared just after World War II, Montale chose rather incongruously to celebrate Gobetti as a bourgeois anti-Fascist, denigrating at the same time the idea that any popular movement could have validly opposed the regime.[11] Fascism was a mass movement, according to the poet, and its success in mobilizing vast support indicated exactly how far the people could be trusted. As with the problem of the political responsibilities of culture, Montale diverged from his admired friend on the topic of elites versus masses. The poet's verse regularly disparages the multitude, who generally seem to him mindless and all too readily recruited to serve evil ends, while only a small band of the elect can be counted on to cherish reason and retain a sense of humanity.

Croce. The same year that *Ossi di seppia* was published, Montale joined with many other intellectuals, artists, and political figures in signing a declaration drawn up by Croce to counter a recently issued "Manifesto of Fascist Intellectuals." The Fascists' document was triumphant in tone, heralding the birth of the Fascist "faith," emphasizing the individual's willing subordination to this exciting new ideal, and discounting as ineffectual the remaining opposition. In his reply, Croce protested this attempt to draft artists and intellectuals to serve political ends. The philosophical system for which he was by then famous (and which he would continue to test and rework) viewed as fundamental the distinction between practical, utilitarian activity on the one hand, and theoretical or artistic activity on the other. It was not that the person of culture should take no interest in politics—Croce himself, as a matter of fact, was a member of the national senate—but the idea that culture itself, art and philosophy, could be nationalized, made instruments of the state—this was repugnant to the philosopher.

Montale undoubtedly approved Croce's stipulation of a distance between politics and poetry. But on other issues, the poet was not always in harmony with this imposing figure, whose vast influence on Italian culture he had acknowledged in "Style and Tradition." In particular, Montale rebelled against Croce's opinions on modernist writing. For the critic had gradually come to feel that all the tradition-breaking art of the late nineteenth and early twentieth centuries had been nothing less than spiritual preparation for Fascism. The fragmentary structures and the predominance of music over sense in some modernist writing, for instance, seemed to him symptoms of the irrational, uncivilized impulses that were to fuel Fascism. The revelling of a part of the avant-garde in the destruction of World War I also testified to the barbarity of these writers. Croce unfolded his thesis about the connection between Fascism and modernism in two circumspectly written books, a history of Italy and a history of Europe, published respectively in 1928 and 1932. After the demise of Fascism in 1945, with the restraints of censorship removed, he would draw up a more explicit indictment of modernism, one that reached back even to Mallarmé and Rimbaud, linking them and many writers that came after to the inhuman reigns of the Nazis and Fascists. Since Croce was not only the most influential literary critic of the day, but also a key anti-Fascist, his charges were impossible to ignore. And because the anti-Fascist Montale felt many affinities for modernist writers, it became pressing business for him after World War II to refute Croce. The defense of modernism will play a crucial role in his postwar essays and poetry.[12]

Florence

To return to *Ossi di seppia:* the book soon made an impression on Italian letters, though the first reactions were not always favorable. After three years it reappeared in a second, enlarged edition, accompanied by a laudatory introduction written by Alfredo Gargiulo, a critic with Crocean affiliations, but respected also for his independence of judgment. Yet Prezzolini, for example, expressed immediate reservations about the collection, dubious as to whether it was really the "revelation" that some took it for.[13] At least its publication, together with articles for literary journals, had gained the poet enough of a reputation to get a job. Montale's dream was to escape from his native Genoa, a city that now seemed to him agonizingly provincial. For a while he had worried that he would never be able to pass beyond the confines of those places where he had spent his childhood and youth. And perhaps he imagined for himself something like the fate of the character in Guido Gozzano's turn-of-the-century poem, "Totò Merùmeni," who saw himself growing old in his family's country house, composing pathetic little verses as consolation for the uneventfulness of his life.[14] But in 1927 Montale was hired by the Bemporad publishing house and could flee, if not to the metropolis of Milan that he longed for, at least to Florence.

The work at Bemporad, which included writing advertising inserts for an almanac, did not last long. Montale quickly found a more satisfactory post, becoming the director of Florence's Gabinetto Vieusseux, a celebrated library that in the previous century had seen such visitors as Giacomo Leopardi and Dostoevski. According to an often-repeated anecdote, Montale received the appointment because he was the only one of the candidates not enrolled in the Fascist Party, a distinction that impressed the mayor of the city, who was no admirer of the new order. The irony was that ten years later the poet would be discharged from his position by a new administration zealously devoted to purging civic institutions of those who were not party members.

During his free hours in the afternoon or evening, Montale was apt to be found at a café known as Le Giubbe Rosse. This establishment, like the Antico Fattore restaurant, became a rendezvous for artists who were not in the good graces of the regime. That is not to say that Montale and his companions were a band of political conspirators. For the Fascist authorities they were malcontents, obstinate in their refusal to participate in the much-trumpeted national culture, but hardly dangerous subversives. Unlike Nazi Germany, Italy under Mussolini often functioned as only a partially totalitarian state; dissident intellectuals, even of the stature of Croce, though harassed and censored, could nevertheless continue to live and work if they were careful not to cross certain bounds. (The more obtrusively recalcitrant, such as Cesare Pavese or Carlo Levi, were exiled to remote areas of the Mezzogiorno, but Montale and his circle were not in this category.) The journal most closely associated with the Florentine dissenters in the early to mid-1930s was *Solaria,* in some ways the continuation of *Il Baretti,* which had been suppressed in 1928.

Among Montale's contributions to the pages of *Solaria* was a review of Charlie Chaplin's *Gold Rush,* a piece that may serve to illustrate the way in which the magazine managed to be out of step with the regime without frontally attacking it. The poet's analysis spoke of the fundamentally Jewish nature of Chaplin's art, and also suggested that the filmmaker's audience was divided into two segments: a mass public that saw movies as pure entertainment, and a few keener spectators capable of grasping the subtleties of the sad clown's art. Here Montale assumes his usual elitist stance, implying that only an elect few will perceive deep meanings and truths. But this antipopular strain is typical of *Solaria*, which, with its circulation of only several hundred copies, prides itself on the isolated position it holds in the none-too-friendly Fascist state.[15]

Moreover, the poet's mention of Chaplin's Jewishness gives a foretaste of sympathies that will figure prominently in his verse. Not too distant was the time when Fascism, emulating the Nazis, would begin a campaign of racial persecution. Then the very name Chaplin would be banned from Italian publications. But when Montale assembled his second collection of verse, *Le occasioni (The Occasions)* in 1939 (he had issued some of these poems in a much briefer book in 1932), it would contain statements of solidarity that the censors evidently failed to understand. A poem of 1938, entitled "A Liuba che parte" ("To Liuba on Her Departure"), spoke of a woman bound for exile, somehow passing unscathed through menacing times. And another piece, the second half of a poem called "Dora Markus," dated 1939, described the flight of the title character, alluding to a similarly ominous backdrop, a "fede feroce," or "savage faith" which the woman might manage to resist.

As Montale informed readers in a postwar note to *Le occasioni*, Liuba and Dora were both Jewish. And though these two figures are minor presences in his poetry and life (Dora seems to have been an amalgam of a woman he never actually met and a passing acquaintance), they are harbingers of an immensely important character who appears in the poet's verse under the name of Clizia. The real woman behind this persona is a member of a prominent American Jewish family. A Dante scholar, she encountered Montale in Florence early in the 1930s. To her the poet eventually dedicated *Le occasioni*, and she appears not only in many of the poems of that collection, but also in much of the verse he wrote in the early 1940s, when the war had forced her to return permanently to America. Gradually, Montale fashions from Clizia something more than just the beloved who is addressed in verse by the enamored bard. In a development that reminds one of Dante's relationship to Beatrice (and "Clizia" is a name from a sonnet attributed to Dante), Montale transforms the woman from a love-object to a fierce angel who combats evil, lending comfort mostly to a select company of followers. As with Liuba and Dora Markus, the poet will make reference to Clizia's Jewishness, insisting on the importance of her heritage. In effect, the plight of the Jews during Nazism and Fascism becomes for Montale a nightmarish proof of the multitude's lack of reason and humanity; and it is Clizia as Jew who incarnates the minority who remain human.

In Florence, Montale also met Drusilla Tanzi, at the time married to the art critic Matteo Marangoni, but eventually to become the companion and finally wife of the poet. Nicknamed "Mosca" ("Fly"), she was an odd little woman full of humors, some of which the poet commemorates in his own fashion in a series of pieces composed after her death in 1963. She is not a powerful angelic presence in his verse, as Clizia is, nor does she evoke from Montale any kind of passionate or romantic love lyrics. If she has an endearing quality it is her eccentricity, her attraction to bizarre and unlikely characters, and her biting, sardonic commentary on people and events. At one point in the 1930s Montale considered leaving Italy and emigrating to America, where he planned to take a teaching job. This departure amounted to abandoning Mosca for Clizia, and the anguish and turbulence generated by the contemplated move were great. The poet finally reconciled himself to staying in Florence with Mosca, but the decision was not a particularly happy one for him. The relationship between the two, both in life and in Montale's poetry, certainly has its moments of asperity. In a ballad set during the nerve-wracking finale of World War II, the poet portrayed himself taking consolation at her bedside (she was then confined to a clinic by a particularly painful disease). But in a piece of 1971, for example, he evoked a less pacific occasion when, shortly before her death, she addressed him with a scurrilous term from Milanese dialect.[16]

Montale once ridiculed biographical critics, suggesting in a delicious satire that, rather than trying to understand the work of Leopardi, these literary detectives would probably have plied the great lyric poet with insipid questions about his love life.[17] Indeed the issues may be confused if one insists too much on taking Montale's work as biography. It is obvious that the Clizia and the Mosca who appear in his verse are not just faithfully rendered pictures of two women. Many times, in fact, Montale relies on literary models in fashioning his characters. Thus Clizia and her successor in the poet's verse, called the fox-woman, are described by him as "Dantesque" (he specifies that he means the two embody an opposition between the angelic and the terrestrial).[18] There is also an obscure figure whose first appearance in his poetry antedates Clizia's; she is named Arletta or Annetta, and the scattered poems dedicated to her suggest that she is a personage with connections to the image repertory developed by the turn-of-the-century writers known as the "Crepuscolari," or "Twilight" generation. Unlike Clizia, the Arletta who appears in Montale's poetry of the 1920s and 1930s is sickly and wan, hardly more than a ghost. She fades before the lyrical speaker can commune with her, and she leaves him helpless and lost. The sense of resignation in these little stories involving Arletta does not permanently satisfy the poet, and he definitely has something other than the "Twilight" vein in mind when he subsequently forges his steely angel Clizia. Part of the appeal and power of Montale's love poetry is the sheer variety of portraits in his gallery and the fact that each figure may contain a complex set of references, whether to literary traditions, to the poet's private life, or to the crises of the historical moment.

Traumatic events filled the closing years of the 1930s for Montale. *Solaria* was ordered to cease publication after battles with the censors over such items as the memoir of a disillusioned young Fascist, a transparently autobiographical piece written by Montale's friend, the novelist Elio Vittorini. For a while the poet contemplated joining the Fascist Party in order to keep his job at the Vieusseux, but the ploy did not succeed and he was relieved of his responsibilities after a humiliating squabble over severance pay.[19] Turning to translation to make money, Montale published versions of Steinbeck, Melville, and Cervantes in the next few years. An anthology of American literature to which he contributed translations of Hawthorne, Mark Twain, Faulkner and others, however, was abruptly suppressed by the authorities. (It would finally be reissued twenty-five years later.) In 1940 Montale published an essay and poems in *Primato,* a journal edited by Giuseppe Bottai, a high functionary in the regime's cultural apparatus. Bottai's intentions and allegiances are still subject to controversy, but it seems likely that his magazine was meant to provide a niche in the Fascist pantheon even for those elements, such as certain modernists, who had been previously intractable to domestication by the regime. At any rate, contributors to *Primato* reserved the right to bite the hand that fed them; Giaime Pintor, for instance, one of its key writers, is also remembered as being among the first to die in the armed resistance to Fascism that arose in the early 1940s.

Some of the poet's companions in this period reproached him for not mounting a more active opposition to the regime. For a younger, *engagé* generation that was to find its vocation in armed struggle against the regime, Montale, together with a whole array of writers of the 1930s labeled "hermetics," now took on the air of escapists, ivory-tower *clercs* who had betrayed their civic duties by confining themselves to narrowly literary pastimes without any attention to the crucial business of current affairs. In his essay for *Primato,* and much more explicitly in postwar commentaries, the poet plays a kind of tightrope game in response to these criticisms, approving neither the artist who stands on the soapbox and broadcasts a political message (this kind of behavior was too D'Annunzian for Montale), nor the writer who locks himself in an ivory tower and cares nothing about the troubles of the day. But a balancing act such as this could not placate all of Montale's interlocutors, and some went away disenchanted with the man and his verse.[20]

In 1943, Montale enlisted his friend, the philologist and brilliant literary critic Gianfranco Contini, to help smuggle a small collection of verse into Switzerland for publication. This clandestine operation was necessitated by the epigraph that the poet had set to his broadside, two lines from the sixteenth-century French poet Agrippa D'Aubigné that provided a not very cryptic commentary on the regime, by then in its death-throes:

> Les princes n'ont point d'yeux pour voir ces grand's merveils,
> Leurs mains ne servent plus qu'à nous persécuter.
>
> Princes no longer have eyes to see these great marvels,
> Their hands now serve only to persecute us.

The booklet was comprised mostly of Clizia poems, devoted to an angel who, like Dora Markus and Liuba, had been put to flight by the forces of evil—but who might survive in a distant refuge and perhaps still transmit messages of sustenance to her faithful. When the Liberation finally arrived, Montale was to republish in his own country these fifteen pieces, together with such other works as "La primavera hitleriana" ("Hitler's Springtime"), a chilling account in verse of the Nazi leader's visit to Florence in 1938.

The Postwar Years

With the destruction of Fascism, long pent-up intellectual and artistic energies were released. Very soon after the liberation of Florence in 1944, Montale began publishing dissections of Fascist politics and culture. For the first and only time in his life he joined a political party, the Partito d'Azione, from whose ranks came Italy's first, albeit short-lived, postwar government. The poet also took part in the organization of an influential magazine, *Il Mondo,* to which he contributed heavily in 1945. But relief at the regime's demise had scarcely taken hold when new controversies sprang up. The government of national unity and the moderately progressive politics of the Partito d'Azione were rapidly supplanted by an all-encompassing polarization of politics and culture, with the Communists ranged on one side and the Christian Democrats on the other. In his poetry Montale adopts tones of highest scorn in alluding to this ideological warfare. He terms the opposing factions "red clerics" and "black clerics," and with his very choice of the noun he expresses contempt for what he saw as the equivalent dogmatism of the two factions.[21]

Artists and writers were given a particular jolt by the transition to post-Fascism. In film and literature a movement known as neo-realism blossomed with stunning quickness, treating the historical events and the social problems of the moment, and violating traditional ideas (including Montale's) about the need for a certain distance between the artist and his material. And in retrospect, the writing of the 1920s and 1930s, even that which could offer anti-Fascist credentials, came to seem inadequate to many. Vittorini, in a 1945 issue of his magazine *Il Politecnico,* denounced the culture of the preceding decades, epitomized for him by Croce and Thomas Mann, which in his view had discredited itself by failing to confront Fascism and Nazism unequivocally, by remaining merely literature or art rather than becoming action.[22] In a letter of 1946 Montale records similar charges lodged against himself. At a conference in Milan, in proceedings he described as "Kafkaesque," the intricate metrics of his poetry was taken as proof by some discussants that aestheticism and not anti-Fascism had been his dominant concern in years past. He too had been among those *clercs* who betrayed their responsibilities.[23]

In an essay of this period that harked back to wartime days with something like nostalgia for the absolutely clear choice they offered between the champions of good and the forces of evil, Montale suggested that the post-Fascist situation had degenerated into a complete muddle. When the battle against Fascism ended, its opponents suddenly found themselves at odds, no longer united by the common enemy.[24] Croce thundered with renewed fury against modernism, the Communists demanded progressive, populist art, and the Christian Democrats, securely in power after 1948, attacked the leftist elements of neorealism. In Montale's poetry, Clizia, the figure who had embodied the clear-cut struggle against the demons of Fascism, slips away. Her place is taken by the Fox-Woman, the poet's cipher for a young woman writer of his acquaintance. This creature appears in Montale's verse as the antagonist of narrow-minded, superstitious Catholicism, and as the vehicle for a cautious homage to Rimbaud (much maligned by Croce), but mainly one feels that she represents a disgruntled retreat from the public, political function of Clizia to a more intimate, personal discourse.

Despite a flurry of contributions to reviews, the poet remained without any fixed position until 1948, when he was hired by the *Corriere della sera,* an influential Milanese newspaper not affiliated with any political party, and long regarded as Italy's journal of record. The circumstances of the poet's entry into the *Corriere*'s sanctums are legendary. Happening to visit the newspaper's offices one day just as news of Gandhi's assassination came off the wire, he was drafted to write a front-page analytical piece on the leader of India's independence movement. The poet's article on the "moral style," the intellectual integrity, and the nonviolent principles of Gandhi met with the approval of the *Corriere*'s editors—perhaps not only for its content, but also because it had been produced with apparent ease under deadline pressure. For the next twenty-five years Montale wrote regularly for the Milanese daily, commenting on cultural and political matters, reviewing books, and composing a series of sketches, often semiautobiographical, many of which were later collected in a volume entitled *La farfalla di Dinard (The Butterfly of Dinard).* From this period come the poet's most wide-ranging disquisitions on literature, with judgments on Eliot, Pound, Hemingway, Auden, D'Annunzio, Pascoli, Gozzano, Gide, Sartre, Camus, Kafka, and Musil, as well as many considerations of classics such as Dante and Boccaccio, and commentaries on writers of the younger generation.

The polemical season in Montale's life did not close with the turbulent postwar years. The poem that opened his fourth collection, *Satura* (1970), gave a capsule history of his times, complete with a jaundiced view of post-Fascism, and also offered still another rebuff to those who could accept only committed art and an *engagé* artist. The paradoxical nature of Montale's enterprise in this piece will be readily grasped: while arguing for the poet's necessary remove from the here-and-now, the poem also delves into that present and its debates. Even from the standpoint of language, the last phase of Montale's verse demonstrates an increased permeability to the contemporary world. The prefix "mini," in vogue in the 1960s, the terms "wiretap," "washing machine," "radar," and "TV" all appear in his late work; in a poem of 1969 he playfully portrays himself as slow to catch up with neologisms, and doubtful about whether to prefer "hovercraft" or "hydrofoil."[25] Yet a certain insulation from the here-and-now also endures in the poet's verse, a persistence of that reserve that marked the so-called "hermetic" poetry composed during the regime. In these late poems Fascism figures as the "Augean stables," oblique words summon up the repressive government installed by the Greek Colonels in 1968, and Pier Paolo Pasolini, a writer and filmmaker whose politics and personality Montale found offensive, enters the poet's verse under the name (of Shakespearean inspiration) Malvolio.

Pervading this last stage of the poet's work is a voice that mocks any claim to systematize the world and human experience. Like the disillusioned Romantics of the Nineteenth Century (of whom Leopardi is probably Montale's nearest kin), the poet refuses to believe in any version of progress. The very title *Satura,* at least in its meaning of "miscellany," expresses this reluctance to see the world operating according to any beneficent plan, or life itself as having any particular aim and meaning. As one of the poems in the collection puts it, history is a "flea market," a random assortment of trinkets and trash.[26] Montale makes fun of Croce's neo-Hegelianism that envisions human events unfolding in an orderly fashion, governed by some sort of organizing "spirit." He scorns the attempts of the Jesuit Teilhard de Chardin to construct a coherent interpretation of mankind by reconciling anthropology and Christianity. And several times he ridicules the Left, by now his pet antipathy, for its fervent belief in the improvement of the human lot. Montale puts no faith in the Communist image of progress, and, continuing the metaphor of his phrase "red clerics," frequently associates Marxists with naive religionists who are always spying Paradise just around the corner.

The figure of Mosca often embodies the acerbic cynicism of the poet's final phase. In his verse she makes jokes about the hellishness of existence, laughs uncontrollably at a pompous testimonial dinner held in her honor, and suspiciously keeps her distance from the representatives of orthodox religion. Yet in the medley of registers and viewpoints that forms Montale's last periods, there is also room for occasional angelic presences, little reminiscences, as it were, of an earlier stage in the poet's work, when Clizia had reigned as the powerful agent of good. In fact, both Clizia and the other central female in Montale's private mythology, Arletta or Annetta, return for several curtain calls, appearing in poems that resemble snatches of interrupted dialogue or long-buried recollections. And finally, *Satura* even yields a suite of love poems, devoted to a fey young woman whom the lyrical speaker hesitantly pursues, always wondering whether his age makes the adventure absurd, but still asking himself whether this encounter in the winter of his life might also have some strange, hidden message of consolation to offer.

Montale treated the honors that he accumulated in his old age largely as embarrassments. According to him, the Nobel Prize for Literature that he received in 1975 was probably a sign of his mediocrity as a poet. (Perhaps he was discomfited, as many have been, by the fact that so many of the indisputably great modernists had failed to win the award, while it had often been bestowed on minor talents.) With characteristic self-depreciation, he spoke in his Nobel Address of poetry as "an absolutely useless product," adding that his own "output," a few volumes of verse together with translations and criticism, could no doubt be considered meager results for a career that had spanned fifty years.[27] This assessment, however, contained something more than just conventional modesty, since "useless" and "useful" were for Montale code words, adapted from the Crocean lexicon and signifying for the poet an opposition between benign art and that kind of pernicious literature developed by D'Annunzio to manipulate the audience in one direction or another. It is odd to find Montale still insisting, as he had in "Style and Tradition" half a century earlier, that poetry should not meddle in the political controversies of the moment. After all, his postwar verse had grown increasingly partisan. Perhaps, then, it was nostalgia for the season of a more "pure" lyrical poetry in his own development that led him to include in his discourse at Stockholm a reading of Joachim Du Bellay's "Odelette des vanneurs de blé." This sixteenth-century French poet of the Pléiade, Montale reminds his listeners, had spent several years at the papal court in Rome, and came away with a great revulsion for the corruption he had witnessed there. The poem, however, speaks of the beloved land he had known as a youth, the Loire Valley. The reasons behind Montale's affinity for this little tale and the poem that accompanies it are not hard to fathom. He too might have been the poet of a landscape, if "the events of an incredible reality"—to borrow a phrase from his postwar verse—had not intervened to tilt the course of his career.[28]

Chapter Two
Ossi di seppia
The Poets Laureate Refused

Contained in the very title of Montale's first book of verse, *Ossi di seppia (Bones of the Cuttlefish)*, is an important clue to his initial direction as a poet. Cuttlefish bones are among the small flotsam left on the beach at low tide by the ebbing Mediterranean—indeed Montale's original title for the book was *Rottami (Flotsam)*—and what could be a less prepossessing label? No epic exploits are advertised, nor sublime tones; only a modest disposition and a muted language. In fact "I limoni" ("The Lemons"), the first poem of the collection (if one excepts a dedicatory poem which will be examined later), opens with the narrator's declaration that he will not travel the same route taken by the "poets laureate." Instead of making his way among plants with illustrious literary associations, he will steer a course through humble, commonplace territory:

> Io, per me, amo le strade che riescono agli erbosi
> fossi dove in pozzanghere
> mezzo seccate agguantano i ragazzi
> qualche sparuta anguilla . . .
>
> (TLP, 17)

> As for me, I love the roads that lead to the grassy
> ditches where in half dried-up
> puddles children catch
> a few skinny eels. . . .

The goal of the vagabond narrator in the poem is a grove of lemon trees. (Nothing exotic in this: lemons are quite usual in the Ligurian landscape.) In that quiet spot he has the premonition that nature is about to yield up a revelation, a truth or even a divine sign. But this tense expectation produces no results. No miracle occurs, and he departs. And yet, in another season, in the city now, he chances one day to glimpse, half hidden in an inner courtyard, the lemon trees with their bright yellow fruit, whereupon

> . . . il gelo del cuore si sfa,
> e in petto ci scrosciano
> le loro canzoni
> le trombe d'oro della solarità.
> (TLP, 18)

> . . . the ice melts from the heart,
> and in our breasts resound
> the songs of
> these golden trumpets of solar light.

Montale's nature poem thus offers just a small token of delight, not a Bacchic revel in a lush landscape. The fragment of sunniness apprehended in the gloomy wintertime city is fit subject for a poet determined not to produce exalted works.

The modest proportions of nature in "I limoni" are a means of disavowing the poets laureate. And the reference to these grandiose writers in the first line of the poem is a dart directed principally at D'Annunzio.[1] Certainly Montale's critical writings, beginning with the essay "Style and Tradition," testify to a long struggle in coming to terms with this predecessor. D'Annunzio, much more than Carducci or Pascoli, the other members of that triad of "illustrious" elder writers whom Montale refuses in his 1925 statement, preoccupies the younger poet, provoking in him both detestation and a grudging acknowledgment of the predecessor's inescapable influence on those who came after him. D'Annunzio, as Montale once wrote, was a "monstrous presence" looming over twentieth-century Italian literature, and something of him inevitably "stuck" to all the poets who followed. (The image is of a gluey, disagreeable substance.)[2]

"Mediterraneo": A Fable of Poetic Influence

In addition to "I limoni," there is an important series of Montale's first collection which treats the theme of the young poet measuring himself against other poetic voices and defining his individuality with respect to the precursor or "father." These nine poems are entitled "Mediterraneo," and are placed at the center of *Ossi di seppia*. In them Montale creates an allegorical account of the poet's grappling with tradition and influence. On the literal level, the contest is between the landsman and the sea, though many times in "Mediterraneo" the identification between the sea and poetic tradition becomes explicit. In one instance the poet, weary and doubtful about his future as a wielder of words, addresses his "father" the sea and takes solace in the fact that he has had at least some part in this vast story, that he has been granted at least some tiny role in the tradition:

> Pur di una cosa ci affidi,
> padre, e questa è: che un poco del tuo dono
> sia passato per sempre nelle sillabe
> che rechiamo con noi, api ronzanti.
> (TLP, 81)

> You have entrusted us with at least one thing,
> father, and it is this: that a bit of your gift
> has passed forever into the syllables
> we carry with us, like murmuring bees.

At another point, the sea is compared to a page from a book and is said to "sing." Though the narrator may have momentary regrets about his difficult apprenticeship to the powerful-voiced sea, yet its song recompenses his trials and loosens "inner knots"—allowing the stripling poet his own expression, one imagines:

> Altri libri occorrevano
> a me, non la tua pagina rombante.
> Ma nulla so rimpiangere: tu sciogli
> ancora i groppi interni col tuo canto.
> Il tuo delirio sale agli astri ormai.
> (TLP, 83)

> Other books I needed,
> not your roaring page.
> But I cannot regret anything: you still loose
> my inner knots with your song.
> By now your ecstasy rises to the stars.

The poet oscillates between two basic sentiments in his confrontation with this overwhelming parent. Either he is thrilled, feeling the breakers as an imperious summons and a heady challenge—or he gazes on the vast, ever-moving expanse of water as proof of his own inadequacy and worthlessness. With scarcely controllable excitement, the lyrical speaker descends to the shore, watching as a bird, a kindred creature, swoops down joyously from the dry, rocky backlands to the beach. Or, in another piece of the series, the poet explores the grottoes sculpted by the surf, and admires their "architetture possenti" and "aerei templi" ("powerful architecture" and "airy temples"; TLP, 77). But "Mediterraneo" also develops the notion of the stripling testing himself against the sea and finding himself pitifully impotent. Instead of inspiring, the sea then seems merely antagonistic, and the lyrical speaker, judging himself too weak to face this enemy, simply surrenders:

> Giunge a volte, repente,
> un'ora che il tuo cuore disumano
> ci spaura e dal nostro si divide.
> Dalla mia la tua musica sconcorda,
> allora, ed è nemico ogni tuo moto.
> In me ripiego, vuoto
> di forze, la tua voce mi pare sorda.
> (TLP, 79)

> At times there arrives, abruptly,
> an hour when your inhuman heart
> terrifies us, and parts company from us.
> Your music is out of harmony with mine,
> then, and your every movement is hostile.
> I retreat within myself, empty
> of strength, and feel your voice become dull.

The poet's weakness in comparison to the sea is represented in several ways. He identifies himself with the principle most opposed to his antagonist, dryness: "Mia vita," he says, "è questo secco pendio" ("My life is this dry slope"; TLP, 79) But from this defeat the lyrical speaker also retrieves a fragile form of victory. The barren slope bursts open, producing a daisy, and with this flimsy emblem the narrator confronts the sea again—faltering, perhaps, but still contending with his opponent. The striving of the young poet is also phrased in plainer terms. In another poem of "Mediterraneo" the lyrical speaker contemplates not a figurative barrenness, but the failure of his creative powers:

> . . . dalla mente
> ci cadrà il tintinnare delle rime.
> Oh la favola onde s'esprime
> la nostra vita, repente
> si cangerà nella cupa storia che non si racconta!
>
> (TLP, 81)

> . . . from our minds
> the tinkling rhymes will slip away.
> And the tale through which our life
> is shown will suddenly
> turn into a gloomy history never told.

And in still another piece, the narrator strains to fashion from his "stento ritmo" and "balbo parlare" ("halting rhyme" and "stumbling speech"; TLP, 84) at least a bit of music that will rival his father's. Try as he might, though, his efforts come to naught, and he ruefully admits that he possesses only "le lettere fruste dei dizionari" and "frasi stancate" ("worn-out letters from dictionaries" and "tired phrases"; TLP, 84).

The close of this story is neither wholly triumphant nor totally defeated. In the last poem of the suite the narrator recognizes the might of the sea and lays his own small claim to significance. Once again, as in "I limoni," the lyrical speaker acknowledges the humble dimensions of his voice. For what he has appropriated from the sea is not the glory and the roar, but rather a low, rasping tone. He took his lesson, he says,

> . . . dall'ansare
> che quasi non dà suono
> di qualche tuo meriggio desolato.
>
> (TLP, 85)

> . . . from the almost soundless
> panting of
> certain of your desolate noon hours.

Having described the paltry part of the sea's voice that he has taken as his own, the poet adds, "a te mi rendo in umiltà" ("to you I humbly surrender"; TLP, 85). Yet this obeissance is not, finally, annihilation; rather, it is the coexistence of opposing elements. The persistent difference between the poet and the sea is given expression in the last words of "Mediterraneo," in which the speaker takes as his identity the image, not of water, but of fire:

> . . . non sono
> che la favilla d'un tirso. Bene lo so: bruciare,
> questo, non altro, è il mio significato.
> (TLP, 85)

> . . . I am
> but the spark of a brand. Well do I know: to burn,
> this and nothing else, is my meaning.

The metaphor may be self-deprecating, since the spark from a burning brand is a tiny blaze, and one whose duration is perhaps brief. From that point of view there is indeed a "surrender" on the part of the narrator. But to conclude the sequence by connecting himself with the element that is the contrary of water also testifies to the poet's resilient individuality—not his abject capitulation.

Several reasons lead one to believe that the parable of poetic influence enacted in "Mediterraneo" has special reference to D'Annunzio. Of his elder Montale once wrote, adopting a metaphor very close to the allegorical terms used in the poems of *Ossi di seppia*, that all successors would have to traverse the formidable D'Annunzio if they wished to reach a landfall of their own.[3] Certainly the power and the allure of D'Annunzio's music were great—worthy of being compared to the might of the sea. Moreover, as a young writer, this bold adventurer had laid public claim to the role of Nietzschean Superman in the domain of art. For D'Annunzio, Nietzsche's Übermensch provides a model of strength and self-assurance—he is one who relishes stimulation and absorbs influence without flinching. And Montale, like many others, was to marvel at the ease with which this Italian Superman appropriated and exploited literary tradition—predecessors, no matter how high their reputation, held no terrors for him.[4] Furthermore, Montale's "Mediterraneo" is not the only poetic account of the day to deal with a younger generation's struggle with the potent precursor's voice. The critic Edoardo Sanguineti has spoken of the so-called "Twilight" poets ("crepuscolari") of the early 1900s, who developed many fables about their weakness and inconsequentiality as writers—basically, he argues, as a response to the magnificence of D'Annunzio. It is an Oedipal battle, Sanguineti suggests, with the "Twilight" offspring bitterly contesting an oppressive sire. This analysis also neatly fits the case of "Mediterraneo," for the narrator speaks at one point of "la rancura / che ogni figliuolo, mare, ha per il padre" ("the rancor / which every son, o sea, has for his father"; TLP, 80).[5] Yet in spite of his accesses of humility—in spite of his taste for an unpretentious foliage in "I limoni" or his identification with the hoarse, unmusical "panting" in "Mediterraneo"—Montale does not descend to the bathos of the "Twilight" poets. While refusing the magniloquence of D'Annunzio, he nevertheless creates a great deal of eloquence of his own. As he once put it, borrowing a celebrated phrase from Verlaine, his first book had sought to "wring the neck of eloquence," even though in the process the poet might find himself evolving a "countereloquence" of his own.[6] And in fact there is a beautiful and powerful voice in "Mediterraneo," emerging almost in spite of the narrator's distrust of the exalted. Consider this apostrophe to the sea, here praised for its music and endowed with an epithet as distant as conceivable from "ephemeral":

> Antico, sono ubriacato dalla voce
> ch'esce dalle tue bocche quando si schiudono
> come verdi campane . . . (TLP, 74)[7]
>
> Ancient one, I am drunk with the voice
> that issues from your mouths as they open
> like green bells. . . .

"Ossi di seppia": The Scorched Earth

The other major subdivision of Montale's first collection bears the same name as the entire work: "Bones of the Cuttlefish." Indeed if one looks at their appearance on the page, these pieces resemble little fragments of drift. Unlike the poems of "Mediterraneo," which are relatively ample (most run at least twenty lines), these are short, spare items, often no more than eight or twelve lines in length. They constitute a practical demonstration, so to speak, of that modest, even cramped poetic voice to which Montale laid claim from the start of the book. And just as the poet alternated in "Mediterraneo" between weakness and exuberance, so in the section "Ossi di seppia" he wavers between joy and desolation—though it is the latter sentiment that relentlessly gains the upper hand and seems to dictate the stunted dimensions of these pieces. Thus the poet may exult at the sunflower that, like the daisy of "Mediterraneo," suggests relief from the scorched land: "Portami il girasole ch'io lo trapianti / nel mio terreno bruciato dal salino . . ." ("Bring me the sunflower, that I might transplant it / in my land burnt by the salt . . ."; TLP, 53). Or he may celebrate the noon hour, as awesome as the vast, open sea of "Mediterraneo":

> Gloria del disteso mezzogiorno
> quand'ombra non rendono gli alberi,
> e più e più si mostrano d'attorno
> per troppa luce, le parvenze, falbe.
> (TLP, 58)

> Glory of the full-spread noon,
> when the trees offer no shadow,
> and the shapes all about
> turn tawny from too much light.

Yet already in the last two lines of this passage one has an intimation of the decay that dominates the series. Immediately after this description of the glorious midday, for example, comes a poem of admonition. Delight and well-being can be only temporary, the narrator warns, and he summons up a favorite theme of *Ossi di seppia*, the deceitfulness of appearances:

> Felicità raggiunta, si cammina
> per te su fil di lama.
> Agli occhi sei barlume che vacilla,
> al piede, teso ghiaccio che s'incrina;
> e dunque non ti tocchi chi più t'ama.
> (TLP, 59)

> Happiness attained—on you one walks
> [as] on the razor's edge.
> To the eyes you are a gleam that flickers,
> to the foot, taut ice that cracks;
> and so let him not touch you who loves you most.

More often than the beauty and power of nature, the lyrical speaker talks of a "male di vivere" ("pain of living"; TLP, 54), or of a world disintegrating and tumbling to ruin. "Il nostro mondo," says the poet, succinct in his dolorous perception, "si regge appena" ("Our world scarcely holds up"; TLP, 65). As one poem puts it, the musician's hand may strive to master the piano keys, the eyes may strain to decipher the notes on the page, but the harmony will not come forth. Or, in the metaphor of another piece, children frolicking in a dried-up stream bed appear to the onlooker as a sign of life springing up from the barren earth; but while this innocent vivacity conjures up the Golden Age, the narrator can only feel grief, recognizing his own remove from that long-ago felicity. He is among the company of the "animi arsi" ("parched spirits"; TLP, 50), as they are termed in still another poem—souls whose happiness and fulfillment have been throttled.

For those who seek to define the mood of an age, this disillusionment will have a familiar ring. After the apocalypse of World War I, images of collapse and withered innocence indeed seemed compelling. So it is perhaps not mere chance that another poet of the era, T. S. Eliot, should offer in "The Wasteland" a vision strikingly close to Montale's scorched terrain and mental anguish. Perhaps even the "fragments" of culture with which the narrator of Eliot's poem attempts to stave off ruin may recall the bits and pieces—not any great whole—which comprise *Ossi di seppia*. Moreover, Eliot's title "The Hollow Men" will doubtless come to mind when the reader encounters the image in Montale's "Ossi di seppia" of a lyrical speaker who is a mere shell, or a coating of whitewash with no substance within. These two poems, one feels, are parallel statements of malaise. Connections such as these are convincing especially if one remembers the affinity attested to by the publication in 1928 of an English translation of Montale's poem "Arsenio" in Eliot's magazine the *Criterion*. And one might also mention the series of articles that the Italian poet dedicated to Eliot over the years. Links between the two writers will surface again in this discussion, but for now it is sufficient to note the similar visions of desolation with which both worked in the 1920s.[8]

Metaphysics and Politics in *Ossi di seppia*

The earliest critics of Montale, writing in the 1920s and 1930s, read much of *Ossi di seppia* as metaphysical poetry. The fundamental motif of the poems, according to one definition, was a "corrosive critique of existence"; and another description had it that the poet's work consisted of two inextricable faces, the "physical" and the "metaphysical"—the evocation of a landscape in the first place, and then a kind of shorthand philosophical commentary—quite idiosyncratic, of course—on these physical features.[9] This insight applies admirably to pieces like "Spesso il male di vivere ho incontrato," which gives in the title line a generalization about the sorrows of existence, and then follows with a sequence of briefly evoked images that function as physical correlates to the initial statement. (Note the harsh double z's, the repeated "glia," and the almost-rhyme incartocciarsi / riarsa, which all serve as deliberately unmelodious binding for these disparate visions):

> Spesso il male di vivere ho incontrato:
> era il rivo strozzato che gorgoglia,
> era l'incartocciarsi della foglia
> riarsa, era il cavallo stramazzato.
>
> (TLP, 54)

> Often I have encountered the pain of living:
> it was the choked stream which gurgles,
> it was the crumpling of the parched
> leaf, it was the fallen horse staggering.

The other stanza of the piece provides no joy to counterbalance the misery of the first strophe. At best, the narrator attains to an "indifference," a kind of stasis that, though not halcyon, at least gives respite from the torment portrayed in the first four lines; and this state too is accompanied by physical corollaries—a statue in the midday stillness, a cloud, and a bird poised high in the sky.

But perhaps one poem above all others in *Ossi di seppia* comes to mind when one thinks of Montale the metaphysical writer. In this piece, the narrator imagines the sudden dissolution of the material world, an event he perceives as both miraculous and terrifying:

> Forse un mattino, andando in un'aria di vetro,
> arida, rivolgendomi, vedrò compirsi il miracolo:
> il nulla alle mie spalle, il vuoto dietro
> di me, con un terrore di ubriaco.
>
> (TLP, 61)

> Perhaps one morning, as I walk in the glassy,
> dry air, I will turn and see the miracle take place:
> nothingness at my back, emptiness behind me,
> and I will feel the terror of the drunken man.

Upon returning to a normal state of consciousness, he finds himself isolated from the others around him who have never experienced this strange void:

> Poi come s'uno schermo, s'accamperanno di gitto
> alberi case colli per l'inganno consueto.
> Ma sarà troppo tardi; ed io me n'andrò zitto
> tra gli uomini che non si voltano, col mio segreto.
>
> (TLP, 61)
>
> Then, as though on a screen, trees, houses and hills
> will suddenly spring up again—the usual deception.
> But it will be too late; and I will go silently on my way,
> bearing my secret among the men who do not look back.

What distances the lyrical speaker from others in this poem is his vision of the irreality of the real world. A metaphysical meditation, to be sure, and one which the authoritative critic Gianfranco Contini identified as the central theme of Montale's early verse. According to Contini, the narrator of *Ossi di seppia* "finds no object in whose reality he can believe." Or more pithily: "Montale has no confidence in reality."[10] Yet this metaphysical question is also at the center of debates between Fascists and anti-Fascists in the 1920s. For one of the cardinal precepts of the Fascist movement is that reality is here to be used, and used it must be. The Fascists pride themselves on their ability to act upon the real world; they have contempt for those who only speculate or theorize. Typical is this scornful gibe pronounced by Mussolini: "Philosophers resolve ten problems on paper, but they are incapable of resolving even one in real life." Praxis is the idol of Fascism, and in order to act, one must have a real world at one's fingertips. It is not surprising, then, that the 1925 Manifesto of Fascist Intellectuals should have impatient words for those who pass their time questioning the nature of reality. The Fascists call for the immediate translation of convictions into action, and those with a less confident and aggressive approach to the world are ridiculed.[11]

Montale's metaphysics is the inverse of Fascism's—as one would expect, since he signed Croce's statement rejecting the Fascist Manifesto. For him there is no reality waiting to be seized and exploited. And the implications of this lack of conviction vis-à-vis the "real" are evident in "Forse un mattino . . .": a narrator alienated from the majority, divorced from those who function in the here-and-now—out of step, in a word, with the Fascists. Indeed one suspects an undercurrent of political meaning in *Ossi di seppia*'s several portraits of the lyrical speaker who is out of synchronization with others. In the following lines, for instance, the crowd hurrying by does not share the pain that registers momentarily on one man's face:

> So l'ora in cui la faccia più impassibile
> è traversata da una cruda smorfia:
> s'è svelata per poco una pena invisibile.
> Ciò non vede la gente nell'affollato corso.
>
> (TLP, 57)
>
> I know that hour when the most impassive face
> is traversed by a harsh grimace:
> an invisible suffering has briefly appeared.
> But the people in the crowded street do not see this.

To show the solitary man entertaining secret perceptions of his own, picturing himself at odds with the multitude, also represents a disavowal of the new ideology. For as the Fascist Manifesto asserts, the individual must henceforth derive every justification for his existence from collective action. Fascism signifies the "sacrifice of the individual" for the sake of a cause that will furnish a new "reason for being."[12] And this is hardly a notion that *Ossi di seppia*'s lyrical speaker would endorse.

The poem most often taken as anti-Fascist statement in Montale's early verse occupies the first page of the series "Ossi di seppia." Vasco Pratolini, for example, adopted the powerful negations of this piece as the epigraph for his novel *Il quartiere (The Neighborhood)*, a work written in the early 1940s and informed by the spirit of an armed resistance to the regime. But in truth Montale's lines have more in common with words that *Ossi di seppia*'s publisher, Piero Gobetti, wrote when he launched his review *Il Baretti* in 1924. Not that Gobetti was always equally pessimistic in his outlook—the editor did promote a positive program that called for a coalition of the intelligentsia and the working class. But most opponents of Fascism were not on the offensive in the mid-1920s, and in his moments of gloom even Gobetti appears less absorbed with his "liberal revolution" than with simply deflating Fascist cockiness. Thus he rejects grand new definitions of the world and "formulas for salvation," arguing instead for a profound skepticism. At this point the regime indeed seems to have monopolized the themes of confidence and conviction, while its antagonists—as the Fascist Manifesto boasted—could offer only negativism and doubts. Admittedly the Fascist claim serves as a rather accurate assessment of Montale's negation-filled poem:

> Non chiederci la parola che squadri da ogni lato
> l'animo nostro informe, e a lettere di fuoco
> lo dichiari e risplenda come un croco
> perduto in mezzo a un polveroso prato.
>
> Ah l'uomo che se ne va sicuro,
> agli altri ed a se stesso amico,
> e l'ombra sua non cura che la canicola
> stampa sopra uno scalcinato muro!
>
> Non domandarci la formula che mondi possa aprirti,
> sì qualche storta sillaba e secca come un ramo.
> Codesto solo oggi possiamo dirti,
> ciò che *non* siamo, ciò che *non* vogliamo.
>
> (TLP, 47)
>
> Do not ask us for the word which would give a shape
> to our formless soul, announcing it with
> letters of fire ablaze like a crocus
> lost in the middle of a dusty field.
>
> Ah the man who goes confidently on his way,
> a friend to others and to himself,
> and does not care that the August sun
> stamps his shadow on the peeling wall!
>
> Do not ask us for the formula which would open worlds to you,
> ask instead for some twisted syllable, dry as a branch.
> This alone we can say to you today,
> What we are *not*, what we do *not* want.

To his audience—to the invisible questioner of these lines—Montale's narrator declines to issue any word of command. The lyrical speaker here is the opposite of a demagogue: he has no stunning conception of the world with which to excite and influence others. This refusal to give direction to listeners reminds one of the poet's 1925 statement "Style and Tradition," with its rejection of art that endeavors to manipulate the crowd. D'Annunzio may have captured an audience with dramatic speeches, both in fictional self-projections and in real life (thus giving a foretaste of Mussolini's demagogic style), but when Montale's speaker mounts to the balcony, he only declares that he has no answers and cannot lead anyone anywhere.

Aside from the narrator and the invisible other with whom he converses, there is a third party in "Non chiederci la parola . . .": the self-assured man. As even the arrangement of the poem on the page suggests, this figure stands apart from the lyrical speaker. He occupies his own compartment, a separate stanza. And certainly his confident progress through the world is at odds with the narrator's negativism. Perhaps even his unconcern at seeing his shadow cast against a wall is meant to contrast with the lyrical speaker's preoccupation with his own lack of form. The self-assured man is on good terms with himself and others, and this fact too invites a comparison with the narrator. For the lyrical speaker does not see himself at ease with others; he is not one to engage others or be engaged by them. Here, in short, one meets another of *Ossi di seppia*'s melancholics, a bleak character full of uncertainties, confronting the optimistic mainstream man who seems never to be troubled by doubts. It is clear, however, that this is not just a clash of personalities or merely a conflict of competing metaphysical systems. The disputes that separate Montale's persona from others are also political—as Gobetti, Croce, and the intellectuals of the Fascist Manifesto would certainly recognize.[13]

Ossi di seppia's Portrait Gallery

Arsenio. In the mid-1920s Montale's attachment to the Ligurian landscape diminishes somewhat, and his poetic world is enlarged by the introduction of several striking human figures. Among these is Arsenio, a name whose rhyme with Eugenio suggests that it is meant to stand for an alter ego of the poet. The word also has a connection with the Italian adjective for "burnt" or "scorched," thus intimating that its bearer will be among those "animi arsi" or "parched souls" who appear in the series "Ossi di seppia"—among the afflicted, that is, and not the robust. Arsenio's tale is told in the poem that carries his name. (It is this piece that appeared in translation in Eliot's *Criterion*.) In a picturesque resort village, he descends toward the shore, passing down dusty streets where, outside the hotels, carriage horses are drawn up, their straw hatted heads ducked against a gusty breeze. He is tempted shoreward by a gathering storm, forecast by distant thunderclaps, the wind in the palms, and a bright branch of lightning. But the fascination of the tempest resides in something more than sensory pleasures, though its sounds and sights are richly evoked. For Arsenio is attracted toward the meteorological spectacle for metaphysical reasons: its tumult seems to break up the regular, monotonous passage of hours and stands for an alternative, better world, into which he hopes to pass. During his progress toward this place of revelation there comes an event, a trivial-significant happenstance, when the seaweed on the beach stones hampers his step. His aspirations to reach the other dimension soar: this may be the strange moment that means escape from the fixity of before, from that "immoto andare, oh troppo noto / delirio, Arsenio, d'immobilità" ("motionless moving, the all too well-known delirium, Arsenio, of immobility"; TLP, 110). The sense of expectancy builds till the deluge begins. At this instant Arsenio, the "burnt one", meets his contrary, the rainwater. But whereas the primordial tradition would conceive this encounter as a festival of fertility and life (rain falling on the parched earth), Arsenio instead finds himself bitterly disappointed. Personified now as a plant, he stretches in vain toward the life-giving moisture, only to face a chilling vision of death:

> . . . giunco tu . . .
> tremi di vita e ti protendi
> a un vuoto risonante di lamenti
> soffocati . . .
>   e ancora
> tutto che ti riprende, strada portico
> mura specchi ti figge in una sola
> ghiacciata moltitudine di morti.
>
> (TLP, 110–11)

> . . . you, the reed . . .
> tremble with life and reach out
> toward a void resounding with suffocated
> cries . . .
>   and then
> everything that takes hold of you again, street, portico,
> walls, mirrors, fixes you in one great
> icy multitude of dead souls.

As in "Forse un mattino. . . ," it is the everyday world, the world of ordinary objects, that eventually reclaims the narrator—and oppresses him. The particular significance of this frozen inferno unfolds only in the last lines of the poem. Arsenio's agony is to realize that he will know no communion with others. A few gestures or a word might slip through to his encapsuled self, but they will only serve to remind him of his isolation and essential deadness:

> . . . se un gesto ti sfiora, una parola
> ti cade accanto, quello è forse, Arsenio,
> nell'ora che si scioglie, il cenno d'una
> vita strozzata per te sorta, e il vento
> la porta con la cenere degli astri.
>
>   (TLP, 111)

> If a gesture brushes past you, or a word
> falls beside you, perhaps, Arsenio,
> in the dissolving hour, that is the sign
> of a choked life that sprang up for you, and the wind
> carries it away with the ashes of the stars.

Like Eliot's Prufrock, Arsenio is a harshly self-critical character, severe toward his own deficiencies and especially toward his inability to act and shape his destiny. He strives to break the chains that lock him into immobility, but then falls back into a realm of frozen fixity. Among the poet's Italian contemporaries there was a lengthy debate about the implications of Arsenio's paralysis. Elio Vittorini, for example, attempted a definition of Montale's verse in 1931, taking "Arsenio" as his point of departure, and concluding that this personage embodied not defeat, but a powerful impulse to live and prevail.[14] One suspects that Vittorini was anxious not to have his friend Montale tainted by association with the passive opponents of the regime, and so extracted more optimism and "virility" (the term is his) from Arsenio's story than were really there. A more realistic appraisal of Montale's alter ego is supplied by Contini, who calls Arsenio a "memorable portrait of the indecisive man who lacks will."[15] One confirmation that Contini's judgment hits the mark comes in Montale's fourth collection of poetry, *Satura,* where in the opening poem Arsenio returns after forty years, still feeling himself incapable of plunging into the active life, and persistently upbraided by an impatient critic for his "abstention" from the world.

Esterina. An earlier poem in *Ossi di seppia* offers the other side of the coin to Arsenio's anemia, in the person of a female character named Esterina. "Falsetto," the piece devoted to her, sketches the young woman in several poses, always as a kind of intrepid, sporting sprite. She is forever looking boldly forward, her visage "proteso a un'avventura più lontana" ("pointed toward a more distant adventure"; TLP, 22). She is compared to Diana the fierce huntress, and stretches out to sunbathe on the rocks, insouciant as a lizard. Or she advances to the end of a diving board, then laughs and leaps fearlessly into the sea. The narrator can only follow these exploits from the shore, feeling himself congenitally incapable of participating in this gaiety and abandon: "Ti guardiamo noi, della razza / di chi rimane a terra" ("We gaze on you, we members of the race / of those who remain on land"; TLP, 23).

"Falsetto" may at first strike one as simply an occasional poem, for it begins with a reference to Esterina's approaching twentieth birthday. Yet one cannot help noticing that if the piece is a sort of birthday wish in verse, the felicitations come infiltrated by certain menacing notes. The narrator summons up a festive peal of bells, ringing in celebration of the happy occasion—but then adds this disquieting metaphor:

> Un suono non ti renda
> qual d'incrinata brocca
> percossa!
>
> (TLP, 22)

> May it not give you back a sound
> like that heard when a cracked jug
> is struck!

Likewise, Esterina's pleasant basking on the shore has scarcely been evoked when the lyrical speaker insinuates an uncomfortable reflection:

> Ricordi la lucertola
> ferma sul masso brullo;
> te insidia giovinezza,
> quella il lacciòlo d'erba del fanciullo.
> (TLP, 23)
>
> You remind one of the lizard,
> lying still on the bare rock;
> your coming-of-age stalks you,
> as menacing as the child's grass snare.

It is indeed rather disconcerting to conceive the young woman's carefree days coming to a close as abruptly as a little grass noose tightening around a lizard's neck.

In scrutinizing Montale, one comes to recognize that his female portraits have multiple meanings, multiple levels. Working from even the slimmest suggestions provided by real-life encounters (the original Esterina was an acquaintance from the period of the poet's Ligurian shore vacations), he forms complex myths in verse that often draw on literary conventions or develop his own metaphysical and political messages. Thus Edoardo Sanguineti quite plausibly finds the female figure of "Falsetto" to be the successor to a species, dubbed the "mulier fortis" or "woman of strength," who may be observed in Gozzano's picture of a fearless ice-skater in the poem "Invernale" ("Winter Scene"). As in Montale's piece, Gozzano's intrepid sportswoman is contrasted with a weak, timorous male standing on the shore. Such an irresolute, feckless persona frequently appears in *Ossi di seppia,* from "Mediterraneo" to "Arsenio," and Sanguineti makes a strong case for seeing this type of character as reaction to the prodigious Superman D'Annunzio.[16]

The lyrical speaker of "Falsetto," from his vantage point on dry land, takes care to distinguish himself from the happy-go-lucky sea creature Esterina, and implies with his insidious metaphors that her dynamic approach to life and her blissful optimism cannot be trusted. To gloss further the doubts that Montale's narrator interjects in "Falsetto," one might turn to a satirical sketch published in Gobetti's *Rivoluzione liberale* in 1923. Here the sporting life of the vigorous younger generation—Fascist youth, one understands—is mocked. The new model citizen exults in the "strenuous life," glories in a "heady felicity," and knows nothing of sober self-examination.[17] Interestingly enough, this slightly flippant piece published by Gobetti runs parallel to the analysis of Fascism that Croce gave a decade later in his influential *History of Europe in the Nineteenth Century*. The generation that had converted so readily to the Fascist movement, in Croce's account, had shown early signs of violence and mindlessness in its addiction to sports, to the active life; these proto-Fascists needed only a little incitement to "toss away the past" and live "dynamically" in the present moment.[18] This, one notes, is precisely the judgment passed on Esterina in "Falsetto": she inhabits the "sorridente presente" (the "smiling present"; TLP, 23), and only the narrator's skepticism casts shadows on that sunny moment of empty-headed exuberance. As sportswoman, moreover, she corresponds to the ideals of an activist mentality that in the Italy of the 1920s had precise political connotations. It is not surprising, then, that Montale's poem should regard this sprite with coolness.

The chrysalis-woman. Other female characters besides Esterina are found in *Ossi di seppia*, most notably in a group of six poems that are placed just before the closing piece of the collection. Here Montale's narrator contemplates not a creature foreign to him, as in "Falsetto," but a feeble, insubstantial woman who acts, so to speak, as a fit companion for Arsenio. The opening lines of the first poem in this sequence may suggest, however, that the poet has at last created one of those nymphs or nature deities that abound in D'Annunzio's *Alcyone*. Unlike the lyrical speaker of "I limoni," who caught barely a glimpse of "divinities" in the lemon orchard, the narrator of the first poem (entitled "Crisalide" or "Chrysalis") finds a burgeoning life-form in his garden, one which excites him to the highest hopes:

> Son vostre queste piante
> scarse che si rinnovano
> all'alito d'Aprile, umide e liete.
> Per me che vi contemplo da quest'ombra,
> altro cespo riverdica, e voi siete.
>
> (TLP, 115)

> They are yours, these meager
> trees that are renewed,
> made moist and joyful at the breath of April.
> For me, contemplating you from this shadow
> another shoot grows green, and it is you.

The aficionados of D'Annunzio might imagine that this image heralds the birth of a creature similar to the famous Ermione of "La pioggia nel pineto" ("Rainfall in the Pine Grove"): a dryad, a Daphne figure, a female who is a veritable collage of natural features, her face like a damp leaf, her hair fragrant as the flowers.

But in "Crisalide" as well, Montale has clipped the wings of D'Annunzian vitalism. For the metamorphosis of the chrysalis-woman turns out to be a failed miracle; hers is the story of a springtime that only momentarily promises renewal. From the flourishing beauty of the garden she falls back into a dreary limbo:

> . . . M'apparite
> allora, come me, nel limbo squallido
> delle monche esistenze; e anche la vostra
> rinascita è uno sterile segreto,
> un prodigio fallito come tutti
> quelli che ci fioriscono d'accanto.
>
> (TLP, 116)

> . . . You appear to me
> then, like myself, in the squalid limbo
> of maimed existences; and your rebirth too
> is only a sterile secret,
> a failed prodigy like all those
> that flower beside us.

After confronting this realm of withered possibilities, the narrator turns toward a second hope. The idea of limbo has already called up theological and Dantesque associations, and in the rest of "Crisalide" Montale develops what he himself once referred to as the "hypothesis of Grace"—a quasi-religious quest for salvation, for some means of escape from the barren place to which he and the chrysalis-woman have been consigned.[19] Reprieve in fact arrives in the form of a ship, the "barca di salvezza" ("vessel of salvation"; TLP, 117), which stands miragelike just off shore, promising a passage to liberty. The lyrical speaker hesitates between two directions, "la libertà, il miracolo" ("freedom, a miracle"; TLP, 117), and the realization that there can be no evasion. As he puts it, "noi andremo innanzi senza smuovere / un sasso solo della gran muraglia." ("We will go on without moving / a single stone in the immense wall"; TLP, 117). The metaphor, one notes, recalls the close of "Meriggiare pallido e assorto" with its oppressive spectacle of the confining wall topped by forbidding shards of glass.

Even at the start, however, the narrator has termed the ship of salvation an "illusion"—wishful thinking. That way out evidently constitutes too fabulous a resolution for the dilemmas of "Crisalide." Instead of the story-book ending that sees the hero and heroine mount a fantastic hippogriff and fly away, the poem finishes with this consolation, just barely extracted from the general grimness of the fate that envelops the narrator and his companion. When the deceptive vision of freedom fades and all again seems hopelessly fixed, the speaker nevertheless manages to frame a wish for the woman's escape to happiness:

> Il silenzio ci chiude nel suo lembo
> e le labbra non s'aprono per dire
> il patto ch'io vorrei
> stringere col destino: di scontare
> la vostra gioia con la mia condanna.
> È il voto che mi nasce ancora in petto,
> poi finirà ogni moto.
> (TLP, 117)

> Silence closes us within its cloak,
> and my lips will not open to speak
> the pact that I yearn
> to strike with destiny: to exchange
> my condemnation for your joy.
> That is the plea that still lives in my heart;
> afterward every motion will cease.

"Crisalide" teems with images that echo those found in other poems of *Ossi di seppia:* the blooming plant as the antithesis of barrenness; the sea as locus of possibility for the landsman; the wall as metaphor for blockade and frustration. An uncharitable critique might even find the piece jumbled, but it has an undeniable importance as a point of origin for the quasi-religious themes that loom so large in Montale's subsequent verse. It is true that the chrysalis-woman never grows miraculous wings, and it seems as much the narrator as she who points the way to salvation (this is *not* a Dante-Beatrice story then), but still, if there is the "hypothesis of Grace" in the poem, then there exists at least the suggestion of a heaven where angels reside, and that is a line of development that will lead to Clizia.

Even within *Ossi di seppia* the story of a tentative, anxious search for grace is repeated several times. For instance, "In limine" ("On the Threshhold"), a short poem which the poet set as introduction to his first collection, compresses into a few lines the essence of "Crisalide"—an orchard depicted as a wasteland rather than a garden of Eden; the vision, just beyond an obstructing wall, of a tantalizing "phantasm" that will offer salvation; and lastly, the narrator's prayer that his companion be allowed to pass beyond the limits of the awful constriction:

> Cerca una maglia rotta nella rete
> che ci stringe, tu balza fuori, fuggi!
> Va, per te l'ho pregato,—ora la sete
> mi sarà lieve, meno acre la ruggine . . .
>
> (TLP, 13)
>
> Search for a broken link in the net
> that binds us, leap out and flee!
> Go, I have prayed that you be given this—now my thirst
> will be easier, less biting my corrosion.

Montale also identified "Casa sul mare" ("The House on the Sea"), another poem from the penultimate section of *Ossi di seppia*, as akin to the spirit of "Crisalide." Here again, the narrator pines for a fabled beyond, and hopes that the woman will by some miracle reach that goal. But this other zone remains as tremblingly evanescent as the distant islands of Capraia and Corsica on the Tyrrhenian Sea's horizon. Not many may be expected to arrive at such an elusive haven—"Penso che per i più non sia salvezza" ("I imagine that for most there is no salvation"; TLP, 122), says the lyrical speaker. Nonetheless he does not surrender totally to despair, and instead seeks to point the way of escape to his friend before he himself expires. As in "Crisalide," the communication between the narrator and his beloved is tenuous and uncertain. Thus the poem concludes with a doubtful sort of leave-taking, hardly any reassurance at all: "il tuo cuore vicino che non m'ode / salpa già forse per l'eterno." ("Your heart, so near, which does not hear me / has perhaps already set sail for the eternal"; TLP, 122).

Arletta. Not far in spirit from "Crisalide" and "Casa sul mare" are four pieces devoted to Arletta, which make up the rest of the group of six. (These, like "Arsenio," were added to the collection when the second edition was issued in 1928.) Among Montale's female characters, Arletta is unique in that she resurfaces again and again throughout his work, a ghostly presence who refuses to be exorcised. She has been an elusive figure for commentators, since only in her later appearances does Montale's verse give her a name. Quite recently, some clever literary detective work has enabled us to identify her in these poems of *Ossi di seppia.* In approaching Arletta, one has the sensation of entering a secret, highly guarded precinct in Montale's imagination—a sensation heightened by the poet's cryptic references in later years to his real-life model for Arletta: a girl he had known in the days of his Ligurian shore vacations, a childhood friend who had died young.

"Incontro," the most impressive of her poems in *Ossi di seppia,* portrays Arletta as a disembodied soul floating in an eerie, almost hallucinatory landscape that could well have been lifted from Dante's *Inferno.*[20] The narrator finds himself confined to this underworld, feels himself encircled by "impallidite vite tramontanti" and "visi emunti, / mani scarne" ("pale, darkening lives" and "sunken faces, / emaciated hands"; TLP, 126). With the kind of helpless desperation that afflicts one in a nightmare, he struggles to locate the woman, trying to assure himself that she always hovers nearby to comfort him. But she never incontrovertibly materializes, until in a strange epiphany he convinces himself that she lurks in spirit form within a pathetic little plant growing on the doorstep of an inn. He stretches a hand toward her, and Daphnelike, she fluctuates for an instant between human and vegetative shapes. Then, abruptly, she vanishes again. He is desolate, but in closing continues to pray for her aid:

>   . . . Prega per me
> allora ch'io discenda altro cammino
> che una via di città,
> nell'aria persa, innanzi al brulichio

Ossi di seppia 43

> dei vivi; ch'io ti senta accanto; ch'io
> scenda senza viltà.
> (TLP, 127)
>
> . . . Pray for me
> then, that I may descend some other road
> than the city street,
> in the gloomy air, amid the swarm
> of the living; that I may feel you near; that I
> may descend without cowardice.

The underworld of "Incontro" is painted in even darker shades than the limbo of "Crisalide," and very little in the way of hope, much less salvation, can be said to lighten the Arletta poem. One can at least observe that "Incontro" represents a further stage in the development of Montale's ever-evolving female figure: now it is the woman who confers solace and courage, for, just the reverse of the prayers in "Crisalide" and "In limine," it is she who is asked at the close of the piece to lend comfort to the lyrical speaker.

Arletta is also present in the short poem "Delta"—though perhaps to call hers a "presence" is already an overstatement. Again she leaves a very faint trace, and it seems that only the narrator's desperation induces him to believe in her. "Tutto ignoro di te," he says, "fuor del messaggio / muto che mi sostenta sulla via" ("Everything about you is unknown to me, except for the silent / message which sustains me on the way"; TLP, 125). The rather contradictory phrase, "silent message," describes very well this absent one who nevertheless succors the lyrical speaker. Unlike "Incontro" or "Crisalide," "Delta" does not really sketch a situation or a story; the poem is resolved, somewhat in the manner of *Ossi di seppia*'s metaphysical pieces, with a physical correlate to the sentiment: the faltering, indistinct presence of the woman merges into the whistle of a tugboat, lost somewhere in a foggy bay.

The somber figure of Arletta will reappear in every one of Montale's later seasons, and while it is premature to speak now of her ultimate importance in the poet's work, we can at least make some preliminary suggestions about her origins and significance. It has been pointed out that clustered around her are many references to the "Twilight" writers, culminating in a piece entitled "Due nel crepuscolo" ("Two in the Twilight"), written about the same time as "Incontro," but not published until the poet's third collection.

Furthermore, Arletta is a deathly character, and this aspect also connects her with the "Twilight" vein, particularly if one follows the suggestion of Luciano Rebay in seeing her as doomed by consumption. (Telltale signs are found in the "umani atti consunti"—"human deeds consumed"—of "Incontro" and the "ultima consunzione del giorno"—"the last waning [literally, "consumption"] of the day" in "Due nel crepuscolo.")[21] Tuberculosis is the classic "Twilight" disease, of which, for instance, Gozzano died. And it is a malady that serves as the physical analogy for the psychology of writers who felt themselves weak and withered.

Deciphering the chrysalis-woman and Arletta. What appeal does the wan, pallid emblem of decline, Arletta, hold for Montale as he writes in the latter half of the 1920s? Rather conspicuous, one might say, is the contrast in *Ossi di seppia* between the vibrant, dynamic Esterina and the wilting shadow-woman. One way of accounting for the coexistence of these two opposing characters in the poet's first collection is in fact to recall that it is a "Twilight" obsession to see the world divided into two camps, the strong and confident versus the weak and weary. In Gozzano's poem "Il più atto" ("The more fit") the poet's brother represents the side of strength, while the writer himself appears as one of those "pale, darkening lives"—to borrow the words of "Incontro": "Adolescente forte, quadro le spalle e il busto, / irride al mio tramonto con chiari occhi sereni" ("The powerful adolescent, square of shoulder and chest, / laughs at my sunset with clear, serene eyes").[22] A world partitioned between the weak and the robust also brings one back to the "Twilight" generation's struggle with the potent D'Annunzio—a contest whose aftershocks are felt many times in *Ossi di seppia*. And to have an idea of the political import of this literary agon, one may consult Croce's 1928 *History of Italy*. This diagnosis of the nation's spirit anatomizes D'Annunzio's faction with its "passion for sports and gladiatorial combat"—and links it to a similarly bellicose politics of nationalism and imperialism. At the other end of the spectrum, Croce perceives a weariness and skepticism personified by such writers as Gozzano.[23] Here one can also insert Montale's Arletta and the twilit backdrop of her poems; instead of an activist temperament, one finds in these pieces a fading figure scarcely able to provide a message of consolation. Nor is it happenstance that Montale should devise the saga of Arletta just at the historical moment when the heirs of D'Annunzio have prevailed. As in the earlier parts of *Ossi di seppia*, the poet works in this cycle with imagery that bespeaks an antagonism to the triumphant new regime. Even the quasireligious motifs—such as the "hypothesis of Grace" in "Crisalide"—that surface in the latter segments of Montale's first collection may be considered to have a political function. (Certainly when one meets the angel Clizia in combat against the devils of Nazism and Fascism it becomes impossible to ignore the dual meaning of the poet's "religion." Of course, this conflation is even less remarkable if one thinks of the idiosyncratic blend of theology and politics in Montale's beloved classic Dante.) In "Crisalide" and its companion pieces, the narrator expresses a yearning for a transcendental space, a beyond that is far removed from the fixed and immutable present. An identical sentiment finds expression in 1924 in the pages of Gobetti's *Rivoluzione liberale*. The author, the literary critic Domenico Petrini, shares the affliction of many of his fellow anti-Fascists, demoralized by the rising tide of the vigorous new order and dolefully resigned to retreat. (Prezzolini, another of Gobetti's contributors, had already offered roughly the same message in *Rivoluzione liberale*.) His own political helplessness is translated into metaphysical terms (the "fixity" of the world), and the only refuge seems to be in religion:

Everything—both the conquered and the conquerors—appears to us governed by the same hard, relentless law which determines and guides it all. Perhaps never before have we felt so powerfully the religious needs of the spirit, and never have we searched so anxiously for a God.[24]

The analogies between this passage and the contemporary "Crisalide" are evident: for Montale's lyrical speaker nothing can be moved in this world, not a single stone in the wall, and he is left to look feverishly for some sign of "salvation" on the horizon—though that grace may in fact elude him. And what of the prayer that closes "Incontro," with its appeal for the courage to descend a road far away from the cities where the living swarm? Here as well, Montale's narrator withdraws from an intolerable present, pleading for just a small token of faith to comfort his retreat.

"Riviere" and the Figure of the Child

Ossi di seppia closes with "Riviere," composed in 1920 and thus one of the earliest of Montale's poems. Ultimately, the poet came to have ambivalent feelings about this coda, and in a commentary on his own work published in 1946, he classified the piece, along with several others from his first collection, as constituting a "premature synthesis and healing."[25] In the wake of all the visions of impotence, disintegration and gloom in *Ossi di seppia*, "Riviere" does seem to display unwarranted optimism. The poem speaks of a child's longings fulfilled, and here at least the frustrations that beset the lyrical speaker in other parts of the book are erased. Instead of the sadly fragmented self that usually appears in *Ossi di seppia*, the narrator of "Riviere" addresses his alter ego as "anima mia non più divisa" ("my no longer divided soul"; TLP, 133). He also imagines it possible to "cangiare in inno l'elegia" ("change into hymn the elegy"; TLP, 133), suggesting not only an upward shift in his mood, but perhaps also an ampler, more confident poetic voice than is found in the rest of the book. The finale of the piece celebrates potentialities, and adopts an image that is the reverse of that aridity and infertility on which the poet dwells in "Crisalide," "Arsenio," or any number of other poems in *Ossi di seppia:*

>   Potere
> simile a questi rami
> ieri scarniti e nudi ed oggi pieni
> di fremiti e di linfe,
> sentire
> noi pur domani tra i profumi e i venti
> un riaffluir di sogni, un urger folle
> di voci verso un esito; e nel sole
> che v'investe, riviere,
> rifiorire!
>
>   (TLP, 133)

>   To be able
> like these branches
> yesterday barren and bare and today full
> of impulses and sap,
> to feel
> we too, tomorrow, amid the perfumes and winds,
> a resurgence of dreams, a mad press
> of voices toward an outcome; and in the sun
> that strikes you, shores,
> to flower again!

Ossi di seppia

This vigorous, joyful peroration is actually not so foreign to Montale as the semirecantation cited above might lead one to believe. When the poet represents Clizia in her glory or the Fox-woman in her moments of animal vitality, his verse will receive similar injections of health and power. But perhaps Montale's distrust of the optimism in "Riviere" can be seen, at least in a first approximation, as one more instance of his refusal of the triumphalism of the 1920s; melancholy remains his preferred mode of anti-Fascism.

"Riviere," with its seeming fulfillment of the desires of the "fanciullo antico" ("long-ago child"; TLP, 132), also furnishes a convenient introduction to the theme of childhood in *Ossi di seppia*. The figure of the child in Montale's first book is no doubt overwhelmed by the many accounts of the mature persona's anguish, but it nonetheless does have a significant role to play in the poet's repertory of images. As one might imagine, children often serve him as emblems of innocence and simplicity. In "I limoni," for example, the boys catching eels are part of a backdrop that is intended to counter the pompous, inflated poets laureate. Montale also uses the category in a special sense when he addresses his fellow Ligurian poet Camillo Sbarbaro as "estroso fanciullo" ("whimsical" or even "bizarre child"; TLP, 31) in the piece "Epigramma" ("Epigram"). Sbarbaro, eight years older than Montale, is the only writer actually named in *Ossi di seppia,* and this familiarity is both a tribute to a friend and mentor from his years in Genoa and a testimony to the fact that this elder does not represent the sort of fearsome, unnameable "father" that one encounters in "Mediterraneo." He is, in fact, the "child," a label that conforms to his modest poetic voice (the titles of his chief collections, *Pianissimo—Very Softly—*and *Trucioli—Shavings—*are indicative). In "Epigramma" the playful youngster is pictured presiding over a miniature fleet of paper boats; to the passerby (presumably adult) the poem urges a kindly disposition toward this make-believe, and a helpful nudge to guide the flotilla into port.

The vignette drawn in this brief piece is idyllic, and the gentle, indulgent homage continues in the other poem dedicated to Sbarbaro, "Caffé a Rapallo" ("Café at Rapallo"), which speaks of the "musica innocente" ("innocent music"; TLP, 29) of a children's street festival. It is worth noting, however, that Montale uses the idea of the child and his toy boats to different effect in other parts of his first book. In a piece from the sequence "Ossi di seppia," the little commander is advised to beach his paper fleet without delay, before a storm overtakes it:

> Arremba su la strinata proda
> le navi di cartone, e dormi,
> fanciulletto padrone: che non oda
> tu i malevoli spiriti che veleggiano a stormi.
> (TLP, 67)
>
> Pull up onto the scorched shore
> the paper ships, and go to sleep,
> little captain: may you not hear
> the evil spirits that sail by in hordes.

It is destruction that dominates this story, not tranquillity and delicate charm: "Viene lo spacco; forse senza strepito. / Chi ha edificato sente la sua condanna" ("There comes the crack; perhaps without a sound. / He who has built hears his condemnation"; TLP, 67).[26]

Moreover, the image of the child is reused on several other occasions in *Ossi di seppia,* not as the winsome creature seen in the poems dedicated to Sbarbaro, but as a contrast to adult disquiet. A group of children cavorting makes the adult passerby feel the pain of his own remove from the age of simplicity and happiness ("La farandola dei fanciulli sul greto"—"The Dance of the Children on the Dry Stream Bed"). And in "Fine dell'infanzia" ("Childhood's End"), an Eden when "il nostro mondo aveva un centro" ("our world had a center"; TLP, 93) comes to an unnerving close, once again, as in "Arremba su la strinata proda," with the arrival of an ominous, eerie storm. As usual, Montale aims for more than just elegant decoration in his description of the weather. The season of childhood represented in the poem is a time innocent of intellectual dilemmas—

> Eravamo nell'età verginale
> in cui le nubi non sono cifre o sigle
> ma le belle sorelle che si guardano viaggiare.
> (TLP, 93)
>
> We were in the virginal age
> when the clouds are not codes or signs
> but beautiful sisters that we watch sail by.

—and the tempest that puts an end to that simple era also brings a mental turbulence: "Giungeva anche per noi l'ora che indaga. / La fanciullezza era morta . . ." ("For us as well the hour of study was at hand. / Childhood was dead . . ."; TLP, 94). The conclusion of "Fine dell'infanzia" indeed makes one think of the mixture of meteorological and spiritual tumult that forms the core of the story of Montale's adult persona Arsenio.

Of course in these various tales of childhood the poet draws on the archetype of youth as a moment of sweet naiveté. But it is also revelant to note that in the literary argot of Montale's day, the word "child" has peculiar resonances, inspired above all by Pascoli's identification of the poet with the "fanciullino"—the "little boy." Pascoli's most important statement of poetics bears precisely that title, and talks of simple, unliterary tastes and an emotional candor as requisites for the writer of verse—though to be less sympathetic, one might characterize this "fanciullino" as limited and provincial (Pascoli was largely a poet of the countryside), and completely unsophisticated as far as erotic interests go.[27] For the "Twilight" generation as well, the child was a congenial identity, even if, in accordance with their unhappy disposition, the "Twilight" poets were apt to see childishness as something of a curse rather than a joy. (After all, it was probably the imposing parent D'Annunzio that made them perceive themselves as children, and puny ones at that.) Thus Sergio Corazzini (1887–1907), in his poem "Desolazione del povero poeta sentimentale" ("Desolation of the poor sentimental poet") offers this self-pitying definition: "Io non sono un poeta. / Io non sono che un piccolo fanciullo che piange" ("I am not a poet. / I am only a little boy who weeps").[28] Montale finds in Sbarbaro the most felicitous qualities of the child; yet, while there is much affection for his friend in the two poems, the fate of children in the rest of the book gives one the feeling (confirmed by Montale's 1920 review of Sbarbaro's poetry) that "Epigramma" and "Caffé a Rapallo" represent a poetic universe that is a bit too confining, a bit too immature for the author of *Ossi di seppia*.[29] In fact, early criticism tended to identify Montale with a "Ligurian school" consisting of Sbarbaro and several other contemporaries—though it soon became evident that this definition was too limited to compass even the poet's first collection.[30]

The child-poet Sbarbaro, as was suggested above, stands at the opposite pole from the terrible father-poet of "Mediterraneo." In effect, Montale differentiates himself from two literary directions in *Ossi di seppia:* the all too powerful poets laureate and the all too weak "children." The contest with the awesome and often fierce father is told with great drama and some bitterness; dealings with the "estroso fanciullo," however, are basically resolved by putting away childish things—turning the little boy's play, in one poem, into a game that is disrupted by a wicked storm, or, in "Fine dell'infanzia," converting childhood into the threshhold of adult confusion and anxiety.

The acts of differentiation or individuation worked out by the poet of *Ossi di seppia* with the metaphors "father" and "child" find a corollary in Montale's essay "Style and Tradition." The laureates with their trumpet-blast messages are disavowed (and here Pascoli, because of his patriotic and socialist verse, is added to the company of the civic bards Carducci and D'Annunzio)—but so too are the excessively meek and self-deprecating poets. Thus Montale asks for a return of poetry to the status of "il decoro e il vanto del nostro paese" ("the adornment and pride of our nation") and an abandonment of verse that is "una solitaria vergogna individuale" ("a shameful practice of solitary individuals")[31] The last words are probably a phrase lifted from Gozzano ("Io mi vergogno / sí mi vergogno d'essere un poeta!"—"I am ashamed / yes ashamed to be a poet!") and in accounting for Montale's distaste here for the "Twilight" writer, one can see once more a refusal of the too restricted poetic voice and the too bathetic self-image.[32] The timid, retiring versifier, portrayed for example in Gozzano's "Totò Merùmeni," constitutes a case of arrested development (Totò indeed has never left the bosom of his family), and this childishness is unpalatable to the more ambitious creator of *Ossi di seppia.*

In the end, just as one finds an ambivalence in Montale toward his immensely gifted "parent" D'Annunzio, so also is there a hesitation in his thinking about the merits or defects of the poet-as-child. Speaking of still another Ligurian writer, Ceccardo Roccatagliata-Ceccardi (1872–1919), Montale expresses a dislike for the academic baggage in this poet's verse, and adds that the fault probably lay with Ceccardo's distrust of the "fanciullo che aveva in sé" ("the child that he had within him").[33] But the child-poet does not always seem to him so estimable. In a commentary of 1945, for instance, he discusses Pascoli's notion of the "fanciullino" and makes it clear that such a program is in the long run inadequate—if poetry is to be great, then "accanto al fanciullo dev'esserci l'uomo" ("by the side of the child must be the man").[34] Keeping these conflicting impulses about the "child" in mind, one returns to "Riviere" with an increased appreciation of the poem's problematic nature for Montale. The jubilant resolution of the boy's desires will be followed (we are speaking chronologically) by what the poet calls the "fall" or "disintegration" of "Mediterraneo": the stripling will turn away from his secure "shores" to face the challenging battle with a mighty father, the sea.[35]

Chapter Three
Le occasioni

The Poetics and Practice of the "Occasion"

Writing to Gobetti at about the time of *Ossi di seppia*'s first edition, Montale commiserated with the editor for the brutal turn Italian politics had taken—the installation of the extremist Roberto Farinacci as secretary of the Fascist Party is the event the poet specifically alludes to—and proposed that Gobetti's entire circle of unrepentant opponents of the regime should go into exile.[1] The publisher's departure and subsequent death in France were in fact not far away; Montale's "exile," however, was to be of a different sort. In 1927, he moved to Florence, and as he put it in a post-regime retrospective, he attempted to live there "with the detachment of a Browning"—like a foreigner residing in a nation whose unpleasant politics he could simply ignore, and also as an artist who could inhabit the world of his writing without paying attention to the reality that lay beyond the margins of his page. But, he adds, such a deliberate abstraction would not suffice in the long run, for the authorities would eventually intervene, depriving the poet of his job—and his sense of blissful remove from the unhappy times.[2]

A chastened note pervades this recollection of the years spent as director of the Vieusseux library and the traumatic moment of severance from that privileged position. Perhaps there is even a trace of postwar revisionism in Montale's retelling, a critique, that is, of the quiet (some would say timid) dissidence he practiced in the 1930s. At any rate, the reference to the political events of that decade is accompanied by an explanation of the writer's evolving poetics in the same period. And here as well it is a question of reticence and an obliqueness gaining the upper hand, not openness and clear proclamations. In form as well, much of the 1930s was marked by involution for the poet. What Montale says he had in mind as he composed the poetry that followed *Ossi di seppia* was "a new method . . . of immersing the reader in *medias res*," a way of suppressing the "occasion," or the circumstantial motivations behind a lyrical impulse, and presenting instead only the end product of the emotions—an objective description.[3] This technique, one feels, basically means cutting away those "metaphysical" statements that are so often paired with the physical illustrations of *Ossi di seppia*. Such a poetics, it should be pointed out, has obvious links to Crocean practice. In an essay of 1921, for example, Croce had offered a reading of Dante's *Divine Comedy* that concentrated on selected passsages held to be "poetic"; the historical and theological messages of the work were meanwhile put in parentheses as not particularly relevant for an understanding of this art. Montale, in an article on Croce, would one day draw a parallel between this sort of procedure and the methods of those modernist writers who sought a "pure" art, uncontaminated by extraneous concerns.[4] And it is plain that, at least to some extent, a similar impulse toward pure lyrical expression motivated many compositions in *Le occasioni*.

In addition, the poet's new *modus operandi* brings to mind T. S. Eliot's "objective correlative," that is, a "set of objects, a situation, a chain of events which shall be the formula of . . . [a] particular emotion."[5] Montale, perhaps working out still another contest of influence, mentions Eliot's doctrine as comparable to his own, but then refuses to acknowledge it as an inspiration for his position. And indeed, with Croceanism permeating the nation's literature and criticism, the idea of distinguishing the lyrical from its documentary source might not have seemed foreign or remote for an Italian writer of the era.

Thus one has a preliminary appreciation of the title Montale eventually chose for his second collection. Indeed many of the poems of the book, including the central series called the "Mottetti" ("Motets"), exemplify the poet's theoretical discourse. One should also note, by way of preface, that several of these "occasional" pieces bear "datelines"—"Verso Vienna" ("Bound for Vienna"); "Lindau" (a city on Lake Constance in Germany); "Nel parco di Caserta" ("In the Park at Caserta," referring to a vast garden, once private and now public, not far from Naples)—that testify to the poet's expanding horizons. In these years he travels frequently, definitively liberated from his childhood cocoon of Genoa-Monterosso. Furthermore, the collection contains poems with English and French settings, and offers epigraphs in Spanish and English, evidence not only of a newly acquired worldliness, but also a European, cosmopolitan viewpoint that makes a sharp contrast with the increasingly strident nationalism of the Fascist state. These occasions that the author seems to stumble upon as he travels consist, in their sparest form, of several descriptive lines, the significance of which may not be readily apparent. "Altro effetto di luna" ("Another Effect of the Moon"), for instance, presents the silhouette of a tree, the commotion as a sailboat sets off from a dock, and a few other images. There is no overt metaphysical message in the eight lines of the poem—no introductory tag, say, about the "pain of living" as in the famous piece from *Ossi di seppia*. If there is a situation or a narrative here, it has been truncated, and if there is a programmatic set of images—like the contrast of barrenness and fertility in the poet's first collection—it is not easily decipherable. The rigorousness of this objectivity may put the reader off; one might even feel remorse that such an acute commentator should sacrifice his messages for the sake of a principle, for a poetry severely confined to description. "Bagni di Lucca" (the name refers to an artists' colony located between Pisa and Lucca) is another piece that works the same limited vein. Autumn scenery occupies this work: the thud of chestnuts dropping to the ground, a wintry chill already in the air, dead leaves spiraling into a ditch. A rustic sight marks the close of the season: "Passa l'ultima greggia nella nebbia / del suo fiato" ("The last flock passes in the fog / of its own breath"; TLP, 147). Here, perhaps because the idea of autumn as emblem of bleakness is so commonplace, one at least intuits a mood, a sentiment.

Among the most startling of these "occasions" is "Verso Vienna," in which the random aggregation of images gives way to a clearly portentous event. The circumstances, as usual in this part of *Le occasioni,* seem to derive from a travel diary: the opening lines sketch a river, and beside it a convent in the baroque style, conjured up by the clever phrase "di schiuma e biscotto" ("foam and biscuit"; TLP, 150). But then the inexplicable occurs, one of those strange, absurd swerves from normality, not unlike the odd happenstance that briefly gave hope to Arsenio. A swimmer emerges dripping from the water and engages the travelers in conversation, indicates the bridge they must cross—then bids farewell and plunges back into the current. This riddlelike encounter is seconded by another: a frolicsome dachshund bounds forth to bark at the tourists, and its cries are characterized in the last verse of the poem as "fraterna unica voce dentro l'afa" ("fraternal, solitary voice in the stifling heat"; TLP, 150). With these final words a hint of the sentiments

Le occasioni

lying beneath the objective surface comes into view. Not so distant from these strange apparitions are the visions of *Ossi di seppia* that fleetingly promise salvation before dissolving. In *Le occasioni* as well the lyrical speaker seeks a token of hope and comfort. That it should appear here in the guise of a "fraternal" dachshund is not so extraordinary, at least in Montale's world. (The animal sign by which the poet recognizes his beloved in the sixth motet is, after all, an even more uncanny one: a pair of "jackals" on a leash.) In the absence of so many other dogmas, with so many methods of faith refused, the poet's steady preference is for the unusual, often the quirky. For Montale's narrator, anxiously groping for the route to transcendence, the eye of the needle seems to be the fluke that emerges unexpectedly from the flow of usual events. These oddities stand at the center of many "occasions," signposts pointing toward a salvation or evasion that the narrator just barely dares to believe in.

Another of these "travelogue poems," "Verso Capua," offers a similarly cryptic moment charged with significance. A river at flood level slows the travelers bound for Capua, and while surveying the inundated landscape the lyrical speaker sees a ray of sunlight pass, then catches sight of his companion in the distance. She is waving a scarf, "la bandiera / stellata" ("the starry banner"; TLP, 154). One might read the sun and stars as conventional emblems of hope and joy, of course—but one can also turn for interpretive aid to the title poem of *La bufera* with its related portrayal of the woman who waves farewell. In the later poem the political import cannot be in doubt. The epigraph of the piece, after all, speaks of bloodthirsty persecutor-princes, and the woman's gesture is the small sign to which the lyrical speaker clings in parlous times. "Verso Capua" dates from 1938, a few years earlier than "La bufera," but for at least one commentator it constitutes an unmistakable part of the cycle that dominates the poet's second and third collections, a cycle devoted to a powerful angel of salvation, Montale's "Jewish Beatrice," inspired by an American woman the poet met in Florence in the 1930s. The scarf that the distant figure waves in the poem may be an article of clothing, but it is also a "starry banner," a cipher for the star-spangled banner of Clizia's homeland—and thus a very particular symbol of comfort for the narrator.[6] In "Verso Capua" the "occasion" scrupulously conceals its background and inspiration, but very soon such reticence will yield to a sequence of transparent allegories that speak of a few dissenters ranged against hostile forces and stormy times.

In a few other places the objectivity of these poems relents and one has an inkling of the ethical and political themes to come in Montale's verse. In "Cave d'autunno" ("Quarries in Autumn") the promise is made that "la bontà d'una mano" ("the benevolence of a hand"; TLP, 148) will return to cut the chill, moonlike landscape; and in "Lindau" a contrast is drawn between the swallow at work building its nest and the ominous flow of dark waters wearing down the river rocks. Intimations, these, of the Manichean struggle between good and evil, light and darkness that will be elaborated in subsequent poems with much greater directness.

The Enchantments of Memory

The oldest of the pieces in the poet's second collection, "Vecchi versi" ("Old Verses"), dates from 1926 and has the marks of being from an earlier phase of Montale's development. In it there is no suppression of the circumstances surrounding the lyrical moment; the poem reads like a little sketch-in-verse, the type of story that in later years might well have been told in the prose of *La farfalla di Dinard*. The scene is set with a wealth of description: a summer evening at the family's villa; the narrator and his mother sitting by the lamplight. Strewn about are playing cards and toy soldiers that recall the diversions of the day. Outside the window a lighthouse beacon flashes, then all at once a terrible winged invader enters:

> Era un insetto orribile dal becco
> aguzzo, gli occhi avvolti come d'una
> rossastra fotosfera, al dosso il teschio
> umano . . .
> (TLP, 142)

> It was a horrible insect, with sharp
> beak, its eyes covered as with a
> reddish photosphere, on its back a human
> skull. . . .

The moth beats frantically around the light, but the tale is interrupted at this point, with one of those abrupt shifts of time that will be favorite devices of Montale the prose writer. The insect has been abruptly reduced to the status of recollected image. Like the familiar faces of relatives or the well-known features of the Ligurian landscape, the creature becomes for the poet only the memory of "una / vita che disparì sotterra" ("a / life that has disappeared beneath the earth"; TLP, 142).

"Vecchi versi" focuses chiefly on the enchantment of remembering. It is "memory," the poem asserts, that holds and nurtures all these bygone things; they have no other life now. Montale here reminds one of Gozzano and the "Twilight" theme of bric-à-brac that has the power to resuscitate the past. Gozzano's "L'amica di Nonna Speranza" ("Grandmother Speranza's Friend"), for example, runs over the clutter of objects in a parlor, then passes to a recreation of a long-ago day when the narrator's grandmother appears as a young girl, just returned from school with a companion.[7] One ought to note, however, that while the "Twilight" poet recalls the past with a wryness and a clever, satirical edge (thus the grandmother and her girl friend gush over their beaux), Montale takes a more somber tone. He wishes to write elegy, and his ghosts from the past have none of the frivolity that Gozzano's do.

It is interesting that even Gianfranco Contini, usually so receptive to Montale's varied impulses and experiments, should find "Vecchi versi" and similar pieces lacking in profundity. Here, Contini says, the poet does not attain real inspiration, but indulges in excesses of evocation.[8] The same analysis might also be applied to "Buffalo" and "Keepsake," both dated 1929, and placed directly after "Vecchi versi" in Le occasioni. The first summons up the spectacle of the noisy, overheated crowd at a Parisian velodrome, an arena where bicycle and motorcycle races are run. As in "Vecchi versi," the climactic moment of the piece comes when the poet recognizes the magic that his own memory can produce. "Buffalo," the mere name of that amphitheater, sets the bright fragments of recollection ashimmer, and around that pretty play of remembering revolves the poem. "Keepsake" as well shows the poet toying with his own ability to evoke; here he conjures up a parade of characters from opera, so many of them stuffed into the twenty-two lines of the poem that they are, as he remarks in a note, "reduced to pure nominal existence, *flatus vocis*" (TLP, 710). A whimsical curio, and no doubt like the leaner occasions, one that serves as a special, private memento. (What memories of performances past do these names hold for the poet who once studied with the maestro Sivori?)

Gerti, Liuba, and Dora Markus

A more purposeful use of recollections and the technique of the "occasion" is found in the poems devoted to Gerti, Liuba, and Dora Markus. "Carnevale di Gerti" ("Gerti's Carnival") swings back and forth between past and present, between the Austrian homeland where the woman's vivid childhood memories lie and the dull garrison town where she now resides in order to be near her soldier-husband. Like the Arsenio who is drawn to "another orbit," Gerti knows the attraction of realms beyond the here-and-now. At midnight on New Year's Eve she follows the custom of her native land and plays the game of dropping molten lead into a bucket of water so as to divine by the strange solidified shapes what ramifications the future will take. And at Carnival time, alone in her room, she goes through the ritual of assigning a little present to each of her friends—though they are all far away. She suffers from nostalgia for the country where she once lived; and that distant place assumes something of the mythical quality that Montale's own childhood haunts often have in his poetry:

> ora chiedi il paese dove gli onagri
> mordano quadri di zucchero alle tue mani
> e i tozzi alberi spuntino germogli
> miracolosi al becco dei pavoni.
> (TLP, 152)

> now you ask for the land where donkeys
> nuzzle sugar cubes from your hands
> and the squat trees sprout miraculous
> shoots beneath the peacock's beak.

(The two verbs in the subjunctive, "mordano" and "spuntino," help to indicate that this country is more dreamland than anything else.)

It is the narrator who gently deprecates Gerti's pretension to live within these fantasies. In the third stanza of the poem he repeats several times the words "Chiedi?" or "Chiedi tu?" ("Do you ask?"), mocking in a kindly way her desire to be borne away to the fabulous other zone. And in the fourth and final stanza, all the magic has been dispelled: the narrator pictures the woman no longer amid those playful illusions, the carnival toys—puppets, rubber balls, and miniature kitchen utensils—but "fra i morti balocchi ove è negato / pur morire" ("amid the dead playthings where dying / is nonetheless denied"; TLP, 153). The spell that Gerti cast over her little gifts has been deflated, and yet she cannot magically disappear herself, but must remain to face the painful detritus of her fantasy world. Glauco Cambon's analogy puts it very well: at the start, "Carnevale di Gerti" portrays an enchanted celebration similar to the festive parade that forms the finale of Federico Fellini's $8\frac{1}{2}$; but at its conclusion, Montale's poem offers a desolate scene of carnival magic dissipated, much like the pathetic close of the filmmaker's *I vitelloni*.[9]

As Cambon also suggests, Gerti's story resembles the chrysalis-woman's. The much sought-after exit from the insupportable present does not swing open, and the narrator and the woman remain amid the "primavere che non fioriscono" ("springtimes that do not flower"; TLP, 153). (The metaphor recalls the language of "Crisalide.") In "Carnevale di Gerti" Montale considers again the "hypothesis of Grace," here represented as "disguidi del possibile" ("misdirections of the possible"; TLP, 153), or odd moments when the impossible retrieval of another time or place actually seems to occur. Memories as salvation? Trinkets, insignificant objects as talismans of highest importance? These are the ruminations suggested by Gerti's nostalgia, and similar questions will occupy many other poems in *Le occasioni*. Noteworthy as well in the concluding lines of "Carnevale di Gerti" is the image of the multitude, in that mundane world to which the woman must return. This "gorgo degli umani affaticato" ("weary whirling crowd of humans"; TLP, 152), like the "swarms of the living" at the close of "Incontro," gives a not very positive view of the mass of men—sets them, indeed, in opposition to a woman who dreams of absent friends in the solitude of her room. In this respect too Gerti's tale points toward future developments in Montale's verse, for these indifferent masses are soon to become in *Le occasioni* a hostile crowd.

"A Liuba che parte" ("To Liuba on Her Departure") is a vignette of eight lines written in 1938. The date is significant, for that year marks the beginning of the systematic persecution of Italian Jews— and, as Montale informs the reader in a note first published in postwar editions of *Le occasioni,* Liuba, like Dora Markus, was Jewish (TLP, 711). The brief poem is a farewell to Liuba, but also alludes to her "family" (perhaps in the sense of "community"?). The woman carries with her a cat, "splendido / lare della dispersa tua famiglia" ("splendid / lares of your dispersed family"; TLP, 155), as the narrator says, charging the household pet with magical-religious significance. The hatbox or cage in which Liuba keeps the animal seems a pathetically flimsy icon, hardly any protection at all, but the poet offers the comforting notion that this little house "sovrasta i ciechi tempi come il flutto / arca leggera—e basta al tuo riscatto" ("rides out the blind times as the flimsy ark / the flood—and is sufficient for your preservation"; TLP, 155). Now the metaphor shifts from Vergilian (the lares or household gods protected Aeneas, the founder of Rome) to Biblical (Noah's ark, with its inevitable connections to the ark of the covenant, the sacred vessel containing the laws given by God to the Hebrews).

It may be that this confluence of images stems from a deliberate irony on Montale's part, since the trappings of ancient Rome appealed greatly to the Fascists, and here the Roman household gods (native, indigenous deities according to most accounts) are mentioned in practically the same breath as the Hebrew symbol. The phrase "blind times," meanwhile, constitutes one of those points of departure for the allegorical language that Montale devises step by step in the 1930s and 1940s to signify Nazi-Fascism. One need only think of *La bufera*'s epigraph with its sanguinary, blind princes to catch the poet's drift.

"A Liuba che parte" is a typical "occasion": it is the "finale of a poem not written," as Montale says in his note, adding that the circumstances that motivated the piece may be selected *"ad libitum"* (TLP, 711). Indeed the very terseness of the composition generates poignancy, just as the fragility of Liuba's baggage makes the journey she faces seem crueler.

A longer and more complex story is told in "Dora Markus," a poem that consists of two parts, the first dated 1926 and the second 1939. The earlier half revolves around those themes of sterility and weariness common in Montale's verse of the 1920s. A "primavera inerte" ("inert springtime"; TLP, 157) sets the mood for these stanzas, followed by the familiar urge to escape this dreariness. Dora leads the way down to the Adriatic shore and points toward her "patria vera" ("real homeland"; TLP, 157); she suffers from a longing for Carinthia, "una dolce / ansietà d'Oriente" ("a sweet yearning for the Orient"; TLP, 157).[10] Rather than refugee as Liuba is, this first part of her poem suggests a Dora who wanders out of restlessness; her enemy, moreover, is an internal one, an existential dilemma:

> Non so come stremata tu resisti
> in questo lago
> d'indifferenza ch'è il tuo cuore.
> (TLP, 158)
>
> I do not know how you endure
> in this lake
> of indifference which is your heart.

And the "amulet" that in the closing lines of the piece is said to save the woman does not assume the same portentous meanings—as lares or ark—attributed to Liuba's belongings. Dora's guardian-emblems are typical items from a woman's traveling case: lipstick, fingernail file, powder puff, and a mouse carved from ivory.

The second half of "Dora Markus," however, introduces a malevolent external force that threatens the woman in much the way that the blind times menaced Liuba. Returned to her native Austria, Dora moves through a placid landscape and staid interiors. Yet in the last two stanzas of the poem the narrator comments somberly that the times grow dark, and while the laurel plant that seasons the cooking retains its evergreen luster, there are also less savory, less beneficent essences in circulation: "distilla / veleno una fede feroce" ("a fierce faith distils poison"; TLP, 160). In this poison-producing "faith" is contained, naturally enough, a reference to Nazism—this much one can learn from Montale's own glosses on the poem—though the choice of precisely that word, "fede," will require some explanation.[11] Suffice it to say for the moment that beginning in the late 1930s the poet's verse develops equations between totalitarianism's manipulation of the masses and organized religion's recruitment of the many. Needless to say, such analogies generate controversy, and upon them have centered some of the fiercest polemics about Montale's work.

The "Motets"

Signs of the beloved. In his note to "Dora Markus" the poet speaks of the imperfect suture between the two sections of the poem, though indeed the whole middle area of *Le occasioni* constitutes a zone of splices and patchwork, testifying to a profound reorientation of subject matter and poetics.[12] Above all, this is the period when Clizia enters Montale's verse as the angel of resistance to Fascism.

Displaced, though not conclusively, is Arletta, the personification of decline and weakness. This shift of outlook can be glimpsed in the two oddly joined parts of "Dora Markus," and appears very conspicuously in the sharp contrast between "Stanze" ("Stanzas"), an Arletta poem dating from 1929, and "Nuove stanze" ("New Stanzas"), a Clizia poem of 1939. The cleft seems even more momentous if one remembers that in 1932 the poet published a provisional second collection, adopting as its title the name of an Arletta piece, "Case dei doganieri" ("The Customs House"); but seven years later the definitive version of his second book would take the title *Le occasioni*—and in postwar editions it would acquire a dedication to the woman who had inspired the Clizia cycle.

Also of composite origin is the sequence of twenty short pieces, called the "Motets," which occupies the center of *Le occasioni*. Here poems of "Twilight" intonation give way to ones devoted to Clizia, and fleeting reminiscences of the bombs of World War I are followed by premonitions of another season of inhumanity on the horizon.[13] These are love poems, dominated by the drama which Montale once defined, in a comment specifically referring to the "Motets," as the usual plight of the lyrical poet: the "absence-presence of a distant woman."[14] Announced in the initial line of the series are the terms of this romantic anguish: "Lo sai: debbo riperderti e non posso" ("You know it: I must lose you again and I cannot"; TLP, 169). Losing, regaining, losing again—the very beginning of the "Motets" plunges the reader *in medias res,* following the standard strategy of the "occasion." And as with the other "occasional" poems of Montale's second book, the emotions are signaled by objective descriptions, bits of landscape, snatches of sound. (As one would expect, given his musical inclinations, Montale cultivates auditory imagery almost as much as visual figures.) Thus the tragedy of separation outlined at the start of the first motet coalesces with gloomy impressions of Genoa's port: a dark springtime, a forest of masts and a screech (of machinery?) that "strazia com'unghia ai vetri" ("tortures like a fingernail on windowglass"; TLP, 169). Part of the poet's evocation of his torment derives from an adept scattering of Dantesque words through these lines; one sees a sort of acrostic emerge, based on the terms "oscura," "selva" ("dark," "forest"), and then the concluding sentence: "E l'inferno è certo" ("And hell is certain"; TLP, 169).[15] Like the confused and demoralized pilgrim who finds himself in the Dark Wood ("selva oscura") in the initial lines of the *Inferno,* Montale's lyrical persona at the opening of the "Motets" confronts an allegory of his pain and loss. Dantesque borrowings, furthermore, recur in this sequence of poems, and it is interesting to contrast the stripling poet's unease before the mighty tradition in "Mediterraneo" with the first motet's confident adaptation of the most famous terms from the most imposing of Italian classics.

In his dismay and bewilderment, Montale's narrator can nevertheless define a quest, a way of liberating himself from his travails: "Cerco il segno / smarrito, il pegno solo ch'ebbi in grazia / da te" ("I see the lost / sign, the single promise I had as a gift / from you"; TLP, 169). Many of the subsequent motets will focus on signs that the lyrical speaker recognizes as emblems of his beloved. In the eighth piece, for instance, the word "segno" or "sign" appears again, this time indicating a sheaf of palm fronds against a wall, a sight which gives the narrator a sudden sense of the woman's presence. (Just why this should be so will be discussed later.) Or, in the eleventh poem, the remembered notes of the woman's singing voice insinuate themselves into the poet's consciousness, even as he speaks with others about subjects far removed from her. But the most celebrated of these manifestations of Clizia (for she is the figure associated with all these signs) comes in the sixth motet. The narrator feels his isolation intensely on this occasion, fearing that he will never see the woman again, when this strange signal greets him, a "barbaglio" or "flash" which he at once understands as a token of Clizia:

> (a Modena, tra i portici,
> un servo gallonato trascinava
> due sciacalli al guinzaglio.)
> (TLP, 174)

> (at Modena, amid the porticoes
> a servant in livery was dragging
> two jackals on a leash.)

This bizarre image was to become a demonstration for Montale's critics of his willful obscurity, his impossibly difficult, hermetic mode of expression in *Le occasioni.* Gargiulo, who had written an introduction full of praise for the second edition of *Ossi di seppia,* recanted and found the poet's next collection practically indecipherable, its "occasions" so recondite as to evoke no response at all from the baffled reader.[16] To such charges as these Montale replied in an acid essay published in the *Corriere della sera* in 1950. He relates the incident behind the poem: his abstracted stroll one day in Modena, an encounter with a servant leading a pair of strange-looking canines on a leash, and the man's deadpan affirmation, upon being asked their pedigree, that the two dogs were "jackals." But then the poet also describes the method in his madness, the means by which the absurd occurrence was transmuted into poetry. Clizia, he knew, loved peculiar animals, so couldn't these "jackals," therefore, be "an emblem, a concealed citation, a *senhal*" of her presence?[17] This line of thinking is not just hocus-pocus or some variant on spiritualism, but refers to a literary tradition that has a special importance for Montale. "Senhal," or "sign," is a term from Provençal, the language of southern France in which were written enormously popular love poems of the late Middle Ages—a strain of love lyric adapted by many poets in other languages, including some of the earliest poets in Italian, among them Dante. The "senhal" was, in its original significance, a code name concealing the identity of the lady addressed by the poet; but Montale uses the word in a broad sense to mean any sort of cipher for his beloved—such as the "jackals" of Modena. So one sees the poetics of the "occasion" merging with elements of the most antique, esteemed tradition of Western European love poetry. Gianfranco Contini, defending Montale from Gargiulo's charges of "obscurity," indeed compared the procedure of the sixth motet with the methods of hermetic love poets in the twelfth and thirteenth centuries—with the difference that in those times the convention of hidden meanings and cryptic references was well accepted both by the poets and their readers![18]

Montale is a very parsimonious craftsman, in the sense that he reuses his poetic materials even as he changes direction and innovates. Thus, while the play of "senhals" denoting the beloved comes to be codified in *Le occasioni* and *La bufera,* these signs also have links with imagery that was already worked out, at least partially, in *Ossi di seppia.* One of the most frequent signals attaching to the female figures of the "Motets" is a light- or fire-sign, as one can see in the dedicatory piece, "Il balcone" ("The Balcony"). Here the afflicted narrator (suffering in the sense that Arsenio suffers, that is from listlessness and hopelessness) encounters the succor that the woman offers. In the first stanza his torpor meets her "certain fire" ("il certo tuo fuoco"; TLP, 137), and from this clash of opposite principles springs, in the middle strophe, a yearning and an energy that he had not known before. The last four lines of the piece then picture the woman straining toward brightness, pointing the way toward the light in an otherwise dark place.

In fact the light and fire of this poem dated 1933 are not completely new in Montale's work, for in "Delta" and "Incontro," Arletta pieces of *Ossi di seppia,* one finds similar flashes and gleams associated with the woman. It has been argued, however, that when the poet adapts these bright signs for Clizia, a new dimension of meaning is created. Like the classic "senhals" of the Provencal tradition, they then conceal a special reference to the woman's real name, Irma Brandeis, which for Montale can be broken down into the components "brand" and "eis," with connections, in the German, to "burning" and "ice."[19] Furthermore, "Clizia," the Dantesque (or at least pseudo-Dantesque) name chosen for the woman, refers also to a mythological character who figures in Ovid's *Metamorphoses* as the beloved of the Sun. The classical myth has her eventually transformed into a sunflower—which brings the chain of citations back to Montale, to the sunflower "crazed by light" in one of the short poems of "Ossi di seppia."[20]

The motif of light surfaces insistently in the "Motets": the "flash" of insight that leads the narrator to see the "jackals" in Modena as Clizia signs; the sheaf of palm leaves "bruciato dai barbagli dell'aurora" ("burnt by the flashes of the dawn"; TLP, 176) in the eighth motet; the vision of Clizia's extraordinary presence emerging like a "lightning bolt" from the clouds in the tenth piece of the sequence. At times one feels that the newly introduced female figure has inherited imagery from a previous period in Montale's verse. Yet Clizia has her own personality, and if she is a stronger presence than her "Twilight" predecessor, it is perhaps not strange to see her associated with lightning, while Arletta's distinctive sign is more often a glimmer of light.

The enemy: machine-age man. This elaborate manipulation of "senhals" would, by itself, be a rather pedantic exercise, but the "Motets" yield much more. For as in many parts of *Le occasioni,* there is both a public and a private element in Montale's discourse, both the troubadour's tribute to his lady and a commentary on the times. Thus in the third and fourth pieces of the series the poet turns back to the trench warfare he endured as a young man, and compares his own trials to those that beset the woman. It is a "Twilight" female who appears in the third motet, confined to a sanatorium where the sick while away long hours playing cards. The narrator's test of survival meanwhile takes place at the front line: he hears the crackling explosions of a new type of grenade and at night witnesses the showers of mortars, like fireworks. Survival is also the theme of the fourth piece, composed about 1939, or five years after the preceding one. This is a Clizia poem, occasioned by news of the death of the woman's father—an event that takes place far away, but nonetheless has its message for the lyrical speaker. Death stalked him as well—the bombs of World War I, the moans of the wounded, the charging squadrons are again summoned up— and yet he escaped. In this motet, however, it is with a special purpose that he survives:

> Il logorìo
> di *prima* mi salvò solo per questo:
> che t'ignoravo e non dovevo: ai colpi
> d'oggi lo so.
>
> (TLP, 172)

> The stress
> of *before* saved me only for this reason:
> I had not met you, and that could not be; beneath the blows
> of today I know it.

Typically enough for the points of juncture in *Le occasioni*, these two adjacent pieces, one devoted to Clizia and the other to a predecessor, harbor somewhat different tendencies. Chance evasion of death is the tale told in the first—an eerie wing brushes past the woman but does not stop; her card has not been drawn from the pack. The Clizia motet, however, speaks of endurance for a reason: first of all for the sake of solidarity between the poet and his distant beloved, and then also as an assertion of *knowing*. "In these difficult present hours," the narrator's final words might be paraphrased, "I know the purpose of my survival, of my persistence." This positive statement, even if of minuscule proportions in the Italian (two monosyllables—"lo so"), nevertheless signifies an important change of direction for Montale's persona, so unbendingly negative from the time of *Ossi di seppia*. And as will shortly be seen, Clizia is capable of eliciting other extraordinary affirmations and certainties from the poet.

The deadly devices of World War I are succeeded in the "Motets" by other sinister mechanisms. In the fifth piece of the series the lyrical speaker bids another farewell to the woman, and the train station where they part becomes the pretext for a singularly disquieting vision of humanity subjugated to a monstrous machinery:

> Addii, fischi nel buio, cenni, tosse
> e sportelli abbassati. È l'ora. Forse
> gli automi hanno ragione. Come appaiono
> dai corridoi, murati!
>
> (TLP, 173)

> Goodbyes, whistles in the dark, gestures, coughs
> and windows lowered. It is time. Perhaps
> the automatons are right. How walled in
> they seem, from the aisles!

When the train starts, its regular mechanical rhythms are an overpowering, terrible sound. Indeed the woman appears as if absorbed into a world where there exist no human beings, only automatons, and no human expression, only the rumble of machinery. (Recall the grating screech that betokened anguish at the woman's departure in the first motet.) Furthermore, the same antithesis between the train and what is human returns in the fifteenth poem, where the narrator says,

> . . . un rumore
> di ferrovia mi parla
> di chiusi uomini in corsa
> nel traforo del sasso. . . .
>
> (TLP, 183)

> . . . the sound
> of a train speaks to me
> of men enclosed, hurtling
> through the tunnel in the rock. . . .

But he wishes to believe that the chillingly mechanical schedule observed by these figures has not everywhere prevailed. There remains another world, one which operates on a timetable where there are "soste ancora umane / se tu a intrecciarle col tuo refe insisti" ("stops that are still human / if you persist in linking them with your thread"; TLP, 183).

In both these motets the woman serves as emblem of what is "human"; hers is a beleaguered resistance to the machine-age man who has lost individuality and reason. The phrase, "perhaps the automatons are right" is a biting paradox made possible by the ambiguity of the Italian idiom: these non-humans may "be right" ("avere ragione") in that they have the upper hand, but they certainly do not possess "reason" (also "ragione"). They appear devoid of that human faculty, and are—as the poet bitterly marvels—locked into their mechanical devices, controlled by them.

Montale's antipathy to the machine, moreover, has precise political implications. Roughly the same wing of the Italian modernists that had rejoiced in the excitement and bloodshed of World War I also found in the machines of the industrial age glorious and beautiful devices. Even before the war the Futurists, for example, had embraced the machine and given a hoot of contempt for every variety of supposedly retrograde humanistic culture. And Croce's *History of Europe in the Nineteenth Century* sees part of the stimulus that produced a baneful "activism" (his code word for Fascism) lying "in the very forces of the modern world, in its incessant emphasis on industrial and commercial enterprises, on technical advances, on the development of ever more powerful machines . . . in its tendency to prefer scientific and practical studies to speculative and humanistic ones."[21] One begins to see the outlines of a "two cultures" debate; and just as the polemic made famous by C. P. Snow in the 1950s had implications for the Cold War, so this Italian version of the *querelle* between technology and humanism is fraught with political meanings. Montale's position on the subject is unmistakable. It will come as no surprise to find him writing disdainfully, in a commentary published in 1931, of those who celebrate the "mechanical civilization of our time."[22] And quite in keeping with his earlier convictions are his frequent postwar diatribes against the excesses of science and technology, which probably herald, as he says in one of his typical pronouncements, the arrival of a "new barbarity."[23]

But a near and present inhumanity looms in the "Motets," personified by the ominous machine-age men and resisted by the few. The eighth piece of the sequence, dated 1938—the same year in which the poem to Liuba was written—associates Clizia as well with her Jewish heritage. The "flashes of the dawn," as Glauco Cambon has written, have to do both with the woman's "sunny nature and with her Palestinian ancestry."[24] It is worth noting also that this motet, after its play with Clizia's "senhals" of fire and ice, concludes with an exceptional instance of communion between the narrator and his beloved, the moment when he feels "sangue tuo nelle mie vene" ("your blood in my veins"; TLP, 176). "A Liuba che parte" most likely carries an ironic charge in its mixture of Roman and Hebrew symbols, and here too—once again in the year that Italy's Nazi-inspired racial laws were promulgated—Montale has his sardonic comment to offer. The law of the land would henceforth prohibit marriages between Jews and members of the "Italian race," but in the poet's imagery Clizia's blood mingles with his own.

No wonder that there should be a sense of isolation felt by the narrator and his companion in these poems of the mid-to-late 1930s. Doubtless it is partly a question of the love story as secret affair, a theme often found in the tradition initiated by the Provençal troubadours. In the eleventh motet, for example, the poet speaks of his "chiusa passione" (literally, "closed," but perhaps also "hidden passion"; TLP, 179) and hears the recollection of her voice touching him even as he talks with "altri che t'ignora" ("others who do not know you"; TLP, 179). When the automatons are described, however, it is clearly a hostile, menacing set of others that is pictured, and likewise in the twelfth poem of the series one reads at least a coolness in the lyrical speaker's comment that the figures around him do not acknowledge his lady's presence. Perhaps the fact that they have been made into "shadows," the opposite of Clizia's sun-emblem, also attests to their suspect nature for the poet. At any rate, the twelfth motet also contains a startling transformation of the woman into angel—along with a reference to the storm she must navigate:

> Ti libero la fronte dai ghiaccioli
> che raccogliesti traversando l'alte
> nebulose; hai le penne lacerate
> dai cicloni, ti desti a soprassalti.
>
> (TLP, 180)

> I free your forehead from the icicles
> that you collected while crossing the high

nebulae; your wings are tattered
by the cyclones, you awaken by fits and starts.

Of course Dante's creation of an angelic creature from the Beatrice of his early love poetry must have been, inevitably, the key precedent for the modern writer—once more Montale exploits an ancient and revered Italian literary tradition in this sequence of verse. A hint of angelic imagery was already present in the tenth motet, where the woman appears as a lightning bolt emerging from a dense cloud; and, given the intricate connections drawn by Dante between Beatrice and light in the *Paradiso,* Montale's inventions, based on Clizia's "senhals" of fire and light, seem even more resonant with significance.

The storm, meanwhile, as the very title *La bufera e altro (The Storm and Other Things)* suggests, will be a fundamental part of the poet's allegory of Fascism resisted. It is worth observing also that the ninth motet speaks of Clizia's amazing powers by borrowing a famous phrase from Shakespeare's *Tempest.* A series of rapidly sketched sights and sounds (a Dantesque image among them) are listed, then the narrator asserts that even if these things are changed into "something rich and strange," the woman at least will not be altered—her mark, or stamp, seems indelible. In Montale's allegories Clizia is recurrently a figure who must maintain her individuality against the onslaught of malevolent forces, and doubtless it was not coincidence that at this point the poet should turn for inspiration in his language to the Shakespearean parable of good and evil revealed by a storm and appropriately rewarded or punished.

Other pieces of the series take up the idea of the tempest, endowing it with apocalyptic qualities. The fourteenth poem portrays a hailstorm that "massacres" the flowers, and the sound of the violent elements merges with the music of another of the motets' mechanical monsters, "la pianola degli inferi" ("the player piano of the infernal regions"; TLP, 182)—even as the woman sings a high-pitched, celestial song. And a description of the countryside beneath a waning sun, in the seventeenth motet, concludes with this frightening vision:

> Con un soffio
> l'ora s'estingue: un cielo di lavagna
> si prepara a un irrompere di scarni
> cavalli, alle scintille degli zoccoli.
> (TLP, 185)

Le occasioni

>   With a gust
>   the hour darkens: a slate sky
>   prepares for the inrush of gaunt
>   horses, for sparks flying from hooves.

Here the image is literally apocalyptic, for as critics have several times pointed out, the sinister animals about to burst upon the sky must derive from the Biblical Horsemen of the Apocalypse.[25]

A flower on the slopes of the volcano. The unnerving end of this poem suggests the mood that prevails in the last motets. It is a finale that shows the poet grasping for the solace of memories, rather than bearing witness to miraculous angelic visitations. Thus the eighteenth piece begins with a plea, "Non recidere, forbice, quel volto . . ." ("Do not cut away, scissors, that face . . ."; TLP, 186), that sounds like the cry of a desperate man left clinging to very slender hopes. Wrested away from him is the image of the woman's visage—the sustenance she gave him. The second stanza of the poem then follows with an objective description that serves as the final, cruel blow: the autumn cold sets in, a tree is felled, and the shell of a cicada drops into the November mud. As though to demonstrate the completeness of the narrator's loss, the next motet represents scenes of springtime—only to finish, once more, with an image of the lyrical speaker's difficulty in making contact with that comfort that the beloved offers. No matter what the season, he seems to be saying, there remains very little of her presence that can aid him: beyond her far-away eyes, he manages to glimpse "solo due / fasci di luce in croce" ("only two / rays of light, crossed"; TLP, 187). The remoteness of Clizia's "senhal" indicates how small the consolation is, an interpretation reinforced by Montale's insistence in a gloss of his own that he meant the cross here to be "a symbol of suffering."[26]

The final motet does register a somewhat different emotional temperature, a bit of tranquillity gained after the vicissitudes of the other poems. The piece begins, ". . . ma così sia" (". . . but so be it"; TLP, 188) and, appearing on the last page of the sequence, these words put a kind of seal over the passions that have gone before, granting the narrator distance from them. In fact the rest of the twentieth motet speaks of souvenirs, remembrances of earth-shaking events now past: a shell with a smoldering volcano painted on its surface, and a coin embedded in a chunk of lava. These are evidently knicknacks on the writer's desk—the fragment of lava serves as a paperweight—and in that sense too they indicate a remove from turbulence and intensity. They are emblems, physical correlates, for "emotions recollected in tranquillity" (to use Wordsworth's famous comment about poetry). Indeed the epigraph to the "Motets," with its vision of a flower clinging to the slopes of a volcano, again suggests passions cooled, and a consolatory token offered to survivors of the tumult.[27]

The poem's last words: "La vita che sembrava / vasta è più breve del tuo fazzoletto" ("The life that seemed / vast is smaller than your handkerchief"; TLP, 188). One thinks of that other "life," the one which gave off "gleamings" in "Il balcone," the piece which is in some sense the point of origin of the "Motets." At the beginning of the cycle there seemed so much promise: an invigorated lyrical speaker strained to join himself to the woman, a wonderful being for him, a purveyor of light. Now, at the end, the possibilities have faded, and perhaps (if this is the reason for evoking the "fazzoletto") all that is left is a farewell wave of the woman's handkerchief, like the wave of the scarf or banner in "Verso Capua." A small gesture, like the little souvenirs on the poet's desktop. It scarcely need be added that the mixture of resignation and somberness summoned up in this close reflects not only the outcome of a love affair, but also the sense of being helplessly present at the beginning of the apocalypse. There are intermittent moments of solidarity and even ecstasy in the "Motets," but departures, disappearances, and a hostile world pressing all around are on the whole the motifs with most weight.

Arletta

The last section of *Le occasioni* recapitulates some of the developments seen in the "Motets" and in the first part of the book: there is a "Twilight" area where the emphasis is on memory and loss, but also the revelation of a decisive Clizia, accompanied by increasingly clear allusions to political events. As in the earlier segments of the collection, these last fifteen pieces range over a period of roughly a decade and are devoted to more than one female figure. Evidently a formal consideration also unites them—as is frequently the case with the subdivisions of Montale's books—for while the "Motets" were short two-stanza poems, this final segment of *Le occasioni* contains longer items.

"La casa dei doganieri," the first piece of the group, returns to the remembered places of the poet's childhood. A customs watchhouse on a Ligurian sea cliff haunts the lyrical speaker's memory, and that desolate, windswept spot becomes, in the hallucinatory language of the poem, a point of rendezvous with a woman long since vanished. The encounter, to be precise, is more wished-for than realized; and it will come as no surprise that the female figure evoked here is the same as the woman of "Incontro" in *Ossi di seppia*. In both these Arletta pieces the desperate narrator searches an eerie landscape for a spirit who never fully materializes. The watchhouse is an ingenious, Kafkaesque rendering of the lyrical speaker's will to commune with the dead woman. This ghostly structure stands at the frontier between two realms, and the narrator contemplates with anguish this point of passage to another zone, pleading piteously for contact with the other side. Another image expresses the futility of his quest: an unraveled thread, of which he holds one end. But unlike Theseus in the Greek myth, Montale's persona is not capable of solving the riddle of this labyrinth, and remains separated from his beloved.

There is a balance in "Casa dei doganieri" between objective description and sentiment that not all the pieces of *Le occasioni* achieve. As the narrator loses his struggle to embrace the woman, for example, one sees the customs house retreat into the distance, fading from memory, while the weathervane on its roof swings "senza pietà" ("without pity"; TLP, 199). The emotion, at this point, seems inherent in the objects. In his recitation Montale also adopts a skillful rhetoric. He begins the poem with the words "Tu non ricordi . . ." ("You do not remember . . ."; TLP, 199) and repeats them in the center and near the end of the composition, making this acknowledgment of the woman's remoteness toll again and again. Meanwhile the narrator's assertion that he still holds one end of the thread leading to her is repeated twice, but within a single stanza and both times immediately discounted; the communion is not to be.

This agonized search for a memory that will miraculously hold, become solid and offer real consolation also appears in "Bassa marea" ("Low Tide") and "Stanze" ("Stanzas"), the next two poems in the sequence. For Montale's lyrical speaker there are few pleasures to be had from this endeavor to recapture the "temps perdu." The recollection of a child's seesaw in a long-ago garden brings back no waves of sweet nostalgia in "Bassa marea," but only a gloomy sense of the irreparable distance between past and present. "Non più quel tempo" ("No longer that time"; TLP, 200) comments the narrator with a terseness that abruptly cuts down any possibility of tender memories. And if the image of the woman persists, it is not contained within any savory cake like Proust's magical madeleine, but in the typically Montalian figure of a lugubrious springtime.

"Stanze," another Arletta poem, varies the theme of an anxious search for communion by constructing the story in terms of anatomy rather than landscape. Thus the opening runs: "Ricerco invano il punto onde si mosse / il sangue che ti nutre . . ." ("I search in vain for the point from which flowed / the blood that nourishes you . . ."; TLP, 201). Like the emaciated faces and hands of "Incontro," these anatomical details suggest the "Twilight" malady, tuberculosis, which has ravaged the woman. And as is typical of the Arletta cycle, the narrator seeks frantically and fruitlessly to have some contact with the woman—while she wilts at his every approach. Some minimal signal does irradiate from her, but these lines of communication are ghostly and insubstantial:

> In te converge, ignara, una raggéra
> di fili; e certo alcuno d'essi apparve
> ad altri: e fu chi abbrividì la sera
> percosso da una candida ala in fuga.
>
> (TLP, 201–2)
>
> In you, unwitting, converges a spoke
> of threads; and certainly a few of these appeared
> to others: and there were those who shuddered in the evening,
> struck by a snow-white wing in flight.

This is hardly a clear and strong message; and the last strophe of the poem finds the lyrical speaker portraying the woman as a halo of ashes that disintegrates and drifts away. (Recall that Arsenio's dashed hopes at the close of his tale were represented by the "ashes of stars" brushed away by the wind.) All traces of the woman and her signals have been effaced, and "Stanze" ends with darkness and damnation engulfing the narrator.

Le occasioni

The weak emanations of Arletta do not permit that kind of extraordinary physical union that one sees in the eighth motet, where the narrator's blood mingles with the woman's—such are the differences between the "Twilight" figure and Clizia. Poems like "La casa dei doganieri" and "Stanze" are well described by Contini's generalization about the usual situation of the early Montale: the poet's search for salvation takes him away from the here-and-now, toward "another world, authentic and internal, or perhaps long-gone, past."[28] To which one must add that the quest is in vain. And doubtless this miserable failure of communion represents, at least in part, a "Twilight" legacy. In contrast to the D'Annunzian persona who seems to make immediate connections with everyone, whether it be the mass audience or the coveted woman, the "Twilight" poet typically feels himself isolated, distant from others. The case of Gozzano's Totò Merùmeni is again instructive: living in premature retirement with doddering, ancient relatives, he is cut off from the rest of the world. His ambitions as a poet have been disappointed, and likewise his dreams of affairs with princesses and actresses. He is, in short, the post-D'Annunzian, fated to be solitary and silent while his predecessor communicated and communed with phenomenal energy. Montale's Arletta poems describe a similar failure of contact, stated, however, in tragic rather than farcical terms. Gozzano's character, after all, deprived of high-society lovers, is content to take the unlettered servant girl to bed. Such ironic details constantly arise in the "Twilight" poet's work, while Montale's cycle is deeply, unvaryingly elegiac.

The "Spanish Interlude"

Like the "Motets," the last segment of *Le occasioni* has a middle ground between Arletta and Clizia, a group of poems dealing with another love and relying on another system of references. One might call this the "Spanish interlude" of the book, for in "Sotto la pioggia" ("Beneath the Rain") and "Costa San Giorgio" ("Saint George's Way"—an avenue leading up to the hillside villas of Florence) there are citations from Saint Theresa of Avila, Cervantes—and a popular Spanish tango of the 1930s. The conjuring power of the word, seen in "Buffalo" and "Keepsake," also propels "Sotto la pioggia," though this latter piece uses the incantatory power as a means to an end—as a route to the beloved. "Por amor de la fiebre" ("For love of fever"; TLP, 203): the narrator quotes these words from the Spanish saint, and their suggestive force—involving, no doubt, the mystic's heady blend of spiritual and physical delirium—brings him in a rush to the contemplation of the woman. Then, in the next stanza, the poet recalls the Spanish lyrics of a tango, heard on a scratchy record: "Adiós muchachos, compañeros de mi vida." (This kitschy line might be loosely rendered, "So long boys, I've loved you all my days"; TLP, 203.) And again he is brought back to thoughts of his love. This poem, moreover, has a conclusion much different from the gloom-ridden Arletta pieces. For in the last lines the lyrical speaker fixes the woman in an image of splendid flight:

> Per te intendo
> ciò che osa la cicogna quando alzato
> il volo dalla cuspide nebbiosaa
> rémiga verso la Città del Capo.
> (TLP, 204)

> Through you I understand
> what the stork dares when, taking
> flight from the foggy pinnacle,
> it wings toward Cape Town.

In "Costa San Giorgio," on the other hand, there is no thrilling vision of the beloved. Instead the poem dwells upon the end of illusions, and the bitter awakening afterward. A will o' wisp of gaslight in the first verse signals the theme of deceptiveness, and then the narrator alludes to the legend of El Dorado, the man of gold whom the conquistadors pursued in their ill-famed adventures. Now this gleaming idol has been dimmed, is captured and tortured on a cross, hangs almost lifeless. And on the heels of this terrible destruction of a beautiful image comes another collapsed illusion:

> Non c'è respiro; nulla vale: più
> non distacca per noi dall'architrave
> della stalla il suo lume Maritornes.
> (TLP, 208)

> Nothing breathes; nothing holds: no more
> does Maritornes take down her light
> for us from the stable's beam.

Maritornes is an ugly servant girl transformed by the demented imagination of Don Quixote into a beautiful damsel smitten by love for him. Here Montale dissolves the enchantment that Cervantes's character so obstinately maintained, repeating at the same time his favorite image of a light that dies—a dream that fades. The poem closes with dismal thoughts: the years passing with a plaintive, mechanical sound, and in the background the figure of the "nemico muto" ("mute enemy"; TLP, 208) tightening the screws of his press—a vague but unmistakably sinister piece of machinery, perhaps related to the evil devices of the "Motets."

"Costa San Giorgio" is a complicated and sometimes obscure poem, weaving together pained outpourings of a despairing lover—a "poem of desperate love," Montale termed the piece—and a network of references bespeaking the end of all bright dreams.[29] As a way of appreciating the mood of the piece, Contini sends the reader back to Leopardi's poem of the early 1800s, "A se stesso" ("To Himself"), in which a similarly embittered narrator denounces the cruel deception of Love and pictures the universe commanded by a "brutto potere," or "ugly power," quite close to Montale's "mute enemy."[30] "Costa San Giorgio" indeed offers a complete reversal of its companion "Spanish" piece, "Sotto la pioggia." The references of the second poem serve not as incantation, but as illustrations of magic powers smashed; and instead of the soaring, daring flight that closes the first composition, there is at the end of "Costa San Giorgio" the dull thud of the "fantoccio / ch'è abbattuto" ("the puppet / which is knocked down"; TLP, 208)—a figure that, whatever its origin, quite obviously signifies defeat and pathos.

Visions of War and Peace

From the pessimism of poems like "Stanze" and "Costa San Giorgio" one passes, in this final segment of the book, to a zone where the woman makes more certain appearances. At the same time visions of evil circulate with ever greater frequency, and a polarity forms that pits the female against the inimical forces. In "Eastbourne," for example, the narrator on holiday in England has persistent intimations of the woman's presence, emerging like flashes of light from the darkness. The wind at the shore is cold, but a beam of light makes the mica cliffs glitter; then the lyrical speaker sees the revolving door of a hotel struck by light, and recognizes a sign of the beloved. In truth her presence is signified also by the anthem "God Save the King," played on the occasion of the August Bank Holiday. "Eastbourne" is dated 1933–35, and as Luciano Rebay has suggested, the link between the cherished companion and a patriotic song whose tune is also adopted by Americans ("My Country 'Tis of Thee") probably has political undertones.[31]

Pleasure at the recovery of the woman's "senhals" is not the only sentiment of the poem, however, for interspersed among these happy returns are grimmer sights. First there is the sad spectacle of the wounded from World War I:

> Vanno su sedie a ruote i mutilati,
> li accompagnano cani dagli orecchi
> lunghi, bimbi in silenzio o vecchi.
>
> (TLP, 210)
>
> The mutilated arrive in their wheelchairs,
> accompanied by long-eared dogs,
> silent children or the old.

And later, perhaps inspired by the revolving door, this ominous image appears, contained in a single line that gains emphasis by its separation from the preceding stanza: "Vince il male. . . . La ruota non s'arresta" ("Evil triumphs. . . . The wheel does not stop"; TLP, 211). Here most likely is an early element of the "prophetic" Montale who speaks of a coming apocalypse, another war. (As the poet himself said of his verse that foreshadowed the impending conflict, "It did not require much to be a prophet.")[32] Thus "Eastbourne," like the "Motets," begins with reminders of the last great war and subsequently gives portents of another doomsday that inevitably approaches: the wheel keeps turning, will not stop.

"Barche sulla Marna" ("Boats on the Marne"), another poem that bears two dates of composition—1933 and 1937—also has the marks of a piece in which a political message is beginning to crystallize. An idyllic day spent boating on the river suggests a dream of peace and goodness, a sort of tranquil progress in which the future holds no terrors. Quite the contrary of that relentlessly turning wheel that brings back a victorious evil in "Eastbourne," the slow drift of the Marne's current signifies happy and orderly times:

Le occasioni

> Il sogno è questo: un vasto,
> interminato giorno che rifonde
> tra gli argini, quasi immobile, il suo bagliore
> e ad ogni svolta il buon lavoro dell'uomo,
> il domani velato che non fa orrore.
>
> (TLP, 213–14)
>
> The dream is this: a vast,
> unending day which pours between the banks
> its gleaming, almost immobile,
> then at every bend the good works of man,
> and a veiled tomorrow which strikes no horror.

There are no explicit references to the fact in the poem, but of course mention of the French river cannot fail to arouse memories of the bloody battles of World War I fought in its vicinity, where tens of thousands of French and German soldiers died in a single day of combat. "Eastbourne" pictures the maimed survivors of the conflict, but "Barche sulla Marna" is occupied by a hopeful vision of peace. Like the two cities on Achilles' shield in the *Iliad*, Montale's two poems offer stark alternatives for mankind: endless bloodshed and violence, or tranquillity and constructive works.

Clizia: Elitism and Mass Movements

Climaxing *Le occasioni* are several Clizia poems of 1939, of which "Nuove stanze" ("New Stanzas") is perhaps the most striking. This piece lies unequivocally in the "prophetic" zone of Montale's work, foreshadowing the war and anticipating the group of poems entitled "Finisterre," which will eventually make up the first part of *La bufera*. The woman figures here as an opponent to a war-machine that has recruited the multitude. The idea was found in the "Motets" and represents the continuation of that antagonism toward the many that was prominent in *Ossi di seppia*. In a postwar gloss, Montale made his point very succinctly: the automatons of the fifth motet were "men understood as mass (and ignorance)."[33] Clizia, on the other hand, will represent an elite few who exercise intelligence and look with loathing upon the mobilization of an all too weak and malleable populace.

Cigarette smoke and a chessboard are the devices with which the poet creates his drama in "Nuove stanze." The delicate arabesques of smoke rising from an ashtray are broken by the ill wind that gusts through an open window. Suddenly the chess pieces are seen against the backdrop of real warriors:

> Là in fondo,
> altro stormo si muove: una tregenda
> d'uomini che non sa questo tuo incenso. . . .
>
> (TLP, 218)

> There in the background,
> another battalion moves: a coven
> of warlocks that do not understand this incense of yours. . . .

The woman alone recognizes the sense of these war maneuvers, while the demonic gathering outside the window does not grasp the meaning of her "incense" (the cigarette smoke). The lyrical speaker hammers at this theme of knowing versus not knowing, and naturally the perceptiveness is all on the side of Clizia, not her foes. The narrator did wonder once if the woman was fully cognizant of the deadly game being played, the "follìa di morte" ("death madness"; TLP, 219) rising everywhere. But in the final stanza of the poem he pays tribute to her wisdom and will, and speaks of an alliance with her powerful presence:

> Oggi so ciò che vuoi;
> . . . resiste
> e vince il premio della solitaria
> veglia chi può con te allo specchio ustorio
> che accieca le pedine opporre i tuoi
> occhi d'acciaio.
>
> (TLP, 219)

> Today I understand what you desire;
> . . . he resists
> and wins the reward of the solitary
> vigil, the one who can turn with you, against the burning glass
> which blinds the pawns, your
> eyes of steel.

These lines are dense with connections to other imagery in Montale's verse. The statement "so ciò che vuoi" recalls the famous negation of *Ossi di seppia,* "Codesto solo oggi possiamo dirti, / ciò che *non* siamo, ciò che *non* vogliamo." *Not* being and *not* willing have been replaced by an assertion of will, a decisive affirmation that constitutes an astonishing departure for Montale's negativistic narrator. The "burning glass," meanwhile, is surely the most fearsome of the diabolical machines in *Le occasioni*—derived, perhaps, from the engine of war that Archimedes was reputed to have designed. Then the "solitary vigil" evokes once more the isolation of a tiny group of resisters, while the "blinded pawns" are another in a long series of disparaging visions of mainstream man in the poet's verse.

As the very title indicates, "Nuove stanze" undertakes a revision of the Arletta poem "Stanze."[34] Indeed the steely-eyed Clizia seems to be a complete reversal of the waning or absent "Twilight" figure. Furthermore, the later piece contains a political message that is remarkably explicit for Montale—it is only a short step now to the poems of "Finisterre," unpublishable in the Italy of 1943. The Arletta cycle, on the other hand, while embodying the anti-D'Annunzian themes of defeat and throttled communication, never becomes specifically political discourse. In effect, the creation of the decisive Clizia of "Nuove stanze" is also a decisive step for Montale, especially since the poet refused for so long any open "engagement" against the regime. The critic Silvio Guarnieri, for instance, records a bitter exchange with Montale in the 1930s, in which he accused the poet of doing nothing to actively help the cause of Anti-Fascism; little ironies about the regime pronounced over coffee were not likely to make the evil vanish. Montale, says Guarnieri, responded with rage to this charge, acknowledging his weakness, admitting himself incapable of any action—and therefore denying anyone the right to reproach him for his aloofness from the fray.[35] In fact Montale, unlike a number of other Italian writers, was to have no career as a partisan; Arsenio never sheds his paralysis and fundamental meekness to the extent that he can pick up a gun. But events and critics were potent enough to alter the course of his poetry, and among the most conspicuous shifts of direction is "Nuove stanze." In its own way the poem signals a high point of activism and commitment for the Montale of the 1930s.

Turning to another Clizia poem of 1939, "Elegia di Pico Farnese" ("Elegy of Pico Farnese"), one might be surprised to see that here the contrast between the few and the many is no longer a question of opposition to a mass organization readily identifiable with Fascism. Instead, the select aristocrats of the "Elegia" confront with scarcely concealed scorn the traditional Catholicism of Southern Italy. And a private revelation that takes place under the auspices of Clizia serves as counterweight to pilgrims celebrating a primitive ritual in the village of Pico Farnese. Old women—"bearded ladies" in the poet's jeering phrase—offer votive candles and candies at a grotto where an ancient sign of the Fish (a Greek symbol for Christ) marks a paleo-Christian shrine. For the narrator of the "Elegia," these rites are "pigra illusione" ("slothful illusion") and the pilgrims' hymns "vano farnetico" ("vain babbling"; TLP, 216). "Slothful illusion" is a particularly cutting description, for its suggests not only the worthlessness of this worship as far as the lyrical speaker is concerned, but also his judgment that such rituals stem only from mental laziness—that lack of intelligence that Montale almost always attributes to the multitude.

The alternative to this simpleminded faith is Clizia, here incarnated as a splendid angel who will discountenance the superstitious old women. Moreover, she will preside over the "trapasso dei pochi tra orde d'uomini-capre" ("crossing of the few amid the hordes of goat-men"; TLP, 216). "Goat-men" summons up the idea of satyrs, and once again the image aims at demonstrating the baseness and stupidity of the many, who are governed by instincts rather than intellect. By contrast, in the final, revelatory lines of the poem, Clizia is represented not only with her usual "senhal" of brightness, but also with the figure of an "eye." The antinomy is plain, and much like that of "Nuove stanze": eyes, vision, insight are properties of Clizia and her few, while the multitude, the pawns or goat-men, are blind, unenlightened.

It is not necessary to make of this violent abuse of primitive Catholicism an elaborate cryptogram hiding a specifically anti-Fascist message.[36] The rustic festivities of Pico Farnese alluded to in the "Elegia" are real enough objects of disdain for the lyrical speaker. There is, however, more to be said about the two-pronged attack of the Clizia poems of 1939, against both the Fascist mobilization of the masses and the ancient religion that holds sway over the simple country folk. One should recall that Italy has no tradition of separation of church and state, and that the Fascists often seemed bent on narrowing the distinction between these two entities even further. Thus the Manifesto of Fascist Intellectuals of 1925 proclaimed the new movement to be a "religion," and Croce, in the counter-statement that Montale signed, felt compelled to condemn this announcement of "the new Gospel, the new religion, the new faith."[37] The poet, moreover, had quite early come under the influence of one of the prime critics of this melding of religion and politics: Gobetti. In 1923, for example, on the occasion of a mass religious gathering at Genoa, one of the contributors to *Rivoluzione liberale* wrote a scathing account of the parallels between Catholic and Fascist ritual, Catholic and Fascist crowd manipulation.[38] Montale as well perceives abominable similarities between the two organizations. His reference to the "fierce faith" of Nazism in the second part of "Dora Markus" bears witness to this—as does the closeness of spirit of "Elegia di Pico Farnese" and "Nuove stanze."

It is worth noting, à propos of the "Elegia," that Montale has a markedly different reaction to his excursion into rural, backward, Southern Italy from many of his contemporaries. Northern intellectuals like Cesare Pavese and Carlo Levi, sent by the regime into internal exile in the Mezzogiorno during the 1930s, found much of value in the archaic native societies—as would the filmmakers Pasolini and Visconti in the postwar years. But this praise for a popular, indigenous culture is not to Montale's taste, devoted as he is to the ideal of a Europeanized, "high" art. And so the native traditions of Pico Farnese are utilized by him, not as examples of wholesome simplicity, but as signs of contemptible simplemindedness. The arrogance of such a position has not escaped some of the poet's critics, and leftists in particular, inspired by Gramsci's championing of a national-popular culture (not to mention the Communist leader's personal sympathies for the Italian South), have found Montale's elitism intolerable.[39]

"Palio," another Clizia piece dated 1939, also balances the woman against the festivities of the masses. The "Palio" is the traditional horse race run in the central piazza of Siena, setting different neighborhoods of the city against one another in a contest known for its tumultuousness. The excited crowd and the parade of ancient banners are recorded by the narrator of the poem; yet much more significant for him is the seal which Clizia holds, as a kind of secret, in her hands. And once again the woman is endowed with special vision, which permits her to see "fuor della selva / dei gonfaloni . . . / oltre lo sguardo / dell'uomo" ("past the forest of banners . . . / beyond the gaze / of man"; TLP, 224). At a thrilling moment of the race the crowd lets loose in unison "un urlo solo" ("a single roar")—but Clizia focuses on another realm, far away from "l'ergotante / balbuzie dei dannati" ("the quibbling / stammer of the damned"; TLP, 224). Indeed Clizia fixes on the living, forgetting both death and these damned beings. One thinks of "La frangia dei capelli" ("The fringe of hair"), a poem of *La bufera,* in which the woman escapes from "le guerre dei nati-morti" ("the wars of the born-dead"; TLP, 240). "Palio" speaks of mock jousting, though soon the conflict will be real. In both cases Clizia supplies the contrary to a mad crowd dedicated to death.

The last piece of *Le occasioni,* "Notizie dall'Amiata" ("News from Amiata") also points toward the next stage of Montale's verse. The first line of this three-part composition portrays the stormy weather that will be the constant metaphor in the poet's work of the early 1940s. And the lyrical speaker lives out this tempest in utter isolation, maintaining only a tenuous contact with the distant woman:

> . . . ti scrivo di qui, da questo tavolo
> remoto, dalla cellula di miele
> di una sfera lanciata nello spazio.
> (TLP, 225)

> . . . I write to you from here, from this remote
> table, from the honey cell
> of a sphere launched into space.

It is "la morte, la morte che vive" ("death, death that lives"; TLP, 227) in this dark, rainy, windy landscape. But if Clizia is far away, there are still occasional signs of her. Most important, coming just at the close of the poem, is this vision, which involves the sort of bizarre beast that the poet tells us the woman loved:

> Si disfà
> un cumulo di strame: e tardi usciti
> a unire la mia veglia al tuo profondo
> sonno che li riceve, i porcospini
> s'abbeverano a un filo di pietà.
> (TLP, 228)

> A mound
> of straw stirs: and, come out at long last
> to unite my vigil with your deep

> sleep which receives them, the porcupines
> quench their thirst at a thin stream of mercy.

The "vigil" of "Nuove stanze" was a much more powerful thing, an alliance with a steely-eyed woman. Clizia is sustenance and comfort for Montale's narrator, but not always lionhearted. Indeed "Notizie dall'Amiata," with its picture of the lonely letter writer and a communication that is mostly telepathic, suggests very well the sense of overwhelming isolation that a certain Anti-Fascist discourse of the 1930s had emphasized. At the conclusion of his *History of Europe in the Nineteenth Century*, for instance, Croce spoke of a scattered band of thinkers and writers who had not surrendered to the dominant mass ideologies of the day (Communism and Fascism) but instead remained devoted to the idea of "liberty." They are, as he put it, "dispersed and isolated, reduced to a tiny, aristocratic Republic of Letters," still determined in their independence.[40] Montale likewise sees his allies as few and distant, while the intervening crowds are hopelessly lost to reason. That is the situation found in the later poems of *Le occasioni,* and it will extend into much of *La bufera* as well.

Chapter Four
La bufera e altro
The Design of La bufera

Like *Le occasioni*, Montale's third collection was assembled over a period of more than a decade, and it is not surprising that its structure should be complex, exhibiting both obvious changes of register and subtle connections. There are two sections, "Finisterre" ("Land's End") and "Silvae" (Latin for "The Woods"), where Clizia dominates, and two parts, entitled " 'Lampi' e dediche" (" 'Flashes' and Dedications") and "Madrigali privati" ("Private Madrigals"), in which another female figure, the fox-woman, appears. Between these longer segments lie two briefer interludes (but one is hardly idyllic, dealing with the tensest moments of World War II); and lastly, a two-poem section called "Conclusioni provvisorie" ("Provisional Conclusions") brings the book to a close.

Very few areas of *La bufera* are innocent of politics. As Contini remarked, the epigraph from Agrippa D'Aubigné at the head of "Finisterre," with its reference to the persecutor-princes, represents nothing less than a "massive and overwhelming invasion" of the "external" world (i.e., politics and history) into Montale's private realm of metaphysical dilemmas.[1] One may wonder just how unheralded this intrusion of politics was, since *Le occasioni* and even *Ossi di seppia* know moments of "engagement," culminating in the poems to Liuba and Dora Markus, and the Clizia pieces of 1939.

In *La bufera* Montale oscillates between his allegiance to a timeless, carefully wrought art, and the ever more pressing need to comment on the events of the hour. The book, therefore, has displays of exacting poetic craft, such as the four sonnets included in "Finisterre," and poems introduced by dates fraught with wartime significance (11 September 1943: Mussolini has been restored to power by the Nazis in Northern Italy). In the years of *La bufera*'s composition the demands of art and those of politics conflict more than ever for the poet, and his verse often strains to control this tension.

"Finisterre": A "Cosmic and Terrestrial War"

Like the "Motets," "Finisterre" centers on the narrator's search for a means of communication and alliance with his far-away love. "Su una lettera non scritta" ("On a Letter Not Written") speaks of his despair at being separated from her and gives the key to interpreting the title of the series:

> La preghiera è supplizio e non ancora
> tra le rocce che sorgono t'è giunta
> la bottiglia dal mare. L'onda, vuota,
> si rompe sulla punta, a Finisterre.
> (TLP, 236)

> Prayers are torture, and, amid the rocks
> uprising, the bottle has not yet reached
> you from the sea. The wave, empty,
> breaks against the point, at Finisterre.

The promontory that stretches toward the New World (where Clizia lives during the war) embodies the speaker's longing for his beloved, but the message in the bottle has not arrived, will not be received.

The gulf between the lyrical speaker and the woman is filled, in "Finisterre," with vivid renderings of apocalypse, resembling those infernal forces and hypnotized crowds seen in *Le occasioni*. In "La frangia dei capelli" ("The Fringe of Hair") the woman escapes, "trasmigratrice Artemide ed illesa, / tra le guerre dei nati-morti" ("Artemis in flight, unscathed, / amid the wars of the born-dead"; TLP, 240). The opponents of the narrator and his companion are these "stillborn" creatures, dehumanized beings, one gathers, like the automatons of the "Motets." And as in his prophetic poetry of the 1930s, Montale creates his Armageddon in "Finisterre" through sound as much as sight. "La bufera" describes a storm with its thunder, hail, and lightning, finally rising to a fever pitch of terrible music:

> e poi lo schianto rude, i sistri, il fremere
> dei tamburelli sulla fossa fuia,
> lo scalpicciare del fandango. . . .
> (TLP, 233)

and then the horrible blast, the ratchets, the throbbing
of drums above the gaping ditch,
the stamping of the dance. . . .

Against this furious tempest the woman's figure is etched: at the end of the poem she turns, waves farewell, and enters the darkness. The storm, it seems, has triumphed, enclosing her in its gloom.

Indeed one may ask what has become of the steel-strong Clizia who appeared in "Nuove stanze," resisting and not relenting against the diabolical war machine. More often than not, "Finisterre" portrays the individual compromised by superior hostile forces. In "Lungomare" ("Seaside Promenade"), for instance, the woman's shadow, cast on a flimsy fence, is distorted as the rising wind sways the slats. "Troppo tardi / se vuoi essere te stessa!" ("Too late / if you wish to be yourself!"; TLP, 235) the narrator exclaims. Here no resolute gaze is turned to face the adversary; all one sees is a pathetically defenseless existence buffeted by the overpowering enemy. As Montale said in glossing the poem, "In the fury of these times the individual will forfeit his own identity."[2]

A similar pessimism dominates the sonnet "Gli orecchini" ("The Earrings"). In this piece the woman is again a tentative presence, not so much leader of a tenacious vigil as another victim in the fated annihilation of all individuals. Against the berserk machinery of war, a pair of human lives matters very little: "Ronzano èlitre fuori, ronza il folle / mortorio e sa che due vite non contano" ("Outside propeller blades are droning, the mad death-rite / drones and knows that two lives do not count"; TLP, 239).

Still another variation on the theme of the individual obliterated is offered in "Serenata indiana" ("Indian Serenade"). The narrator imagines the woman and imagines that she might imagine him as well—but then this tenuous, unreal communication collapses, replaced by a sinister creature that takes possession of the lady and obscures her:

Il polipo che insinua
tentacoli d'inchiostro tra gli scogli
può servirsi di te. Tu gli appartieni

e non lo sai. Sei lui, ti credi te.

(TLP, 238)

The polyp that snakes
inky tentacles among the rocks
can use you. You belong to him,

and you do not know it. You are he, you think you are yourself.

The woman is preyed upon, and does not even realize that she is no longer mistress of her fate. The lack of knowledge in the female constitutes a crucial about-face: while "Nuove stanze" insisted on the woman's perfect awareness, "Serenata indiana" portrays an ignorance that underscores the individual's helplessness.

"Finisterre" is not a place of relieved gloom, however. In these poems Montale also makes further sketches for his portrait of an angelic female, a savior. In "Il ventaglio" ("The Fan") she appears with her characteristic signs (brightness, angel plumage) against the spectacle of mass death:

> . . . la calanca
> vertiginosa inghiotte ancora vittime
> ma le tue piume sulle guance sbiancano
> e il giorno è forse salvo.
> (TLP, 243)

> . . . the dizzying
> chasm swallows more victims,
> but your feathers glow on your cheeks
> and the day is perhaps saved.

Yet the salvation here is qualified by a "perhaps." Furthermore, the closing words of the poem suggest that the day of peace may be attained only through death. "Muore chi ti riconosce?" ("Does he who recognizes you die?"; TLP, 243) the lyrical speaker asks, as though he did not believe there could be any other route for the faithful followers of his lady.[3] Likewise in "Il giglio rosso" ("The Red Lily") the narrator mixes intimations of redemption with ideas of sacrifice and death. The red lily of the title, symbol of the city of Florence where the poet met the lady, sends its roots into her heart; and this is a "trapianto felice" ("happy transplant"; TLP, 242). But in the second half of the piece, the woman is far away, in a cold land, and the flower has been "sacrificed." By the end its blossom unfolds again, though in a world beyond time, where a "celestial harp" sounds and death seems a friendly presence. The sequence of events in the poem thus imitates not only life cycles in the natural world, but also the archetypal Christian pathway: life, death, resurrection.

Generally in "Finisterre" the solidarity between the woman and the narrator—if it exists at all—is consummated beneath the sign of sacrifice. When, in "La bufera," the storm's lightning fixes the landscape in a vivid flash, the lady carries within her this apocalyptic instant, "per tua condanna" ("as your sentence"; TLP, 233) as the lyrical speaker says. Yet this terrible light that "condemns" her also "links" the woman to her companion, betokening their alliance. Moreover, the fearsome brightness that descends onto the trees and walls is connected, in the incredibly compressed imagery of the poem, with both "manna" and "destruction" both a saving gift from God and a devastation.[4] Salvation and annihilation unite, two sides of the same coin. Quite consonant with the foregoing is the conclusion of the poem, balanced as it is between the woman's wave—her gesture of communion with the narrator—and the darkness that envelops her, blots out her figure. Consolation emerges only from obliteration; "persistenza è solo estinzione" ("persistence is merely extinction"; TLP, 320) as a later piece of *La bufera,* "Piccolo testamento," has it.

Perhaps the most optimistic version of the woman's redemptive powers comes in "La frangia dei capelli." This sonnet is indeed a paean to the comfort she furnishes and the generosity of her spirit. That feature of hers described in the title of the piece becomes for the narrator the "whole of heaven," or the wings on which she soars, or "la cortina che gl'indulti / tuoi distendono" ("the cloak which your forgiveness / spreads wide"; TLP, 240). And at the close, her forehead merges with the hopeful dawn. For once, the woman's succor is not overwhelmed by spectacles of extinction, and her powerful benevolence is reflected in an unbroken string of positive images, quite exceptional for "Finisterre."

The dead are legion in this first part of *La bufera:* the born-dead of "La frangia dei capelli," who are objects of the narrator's irony and scorn; the yawning mass grave of "Il ventaglio." In "Finisterre" one also encounters the poet's own dead, family members, ancient servants, and even household pets. Summoning up those who have passed to another world, the narrator performs an act of piety, but also implies a contrast between the dead that remain alive for him, and, on the other hand, the living dead, the faceless hordes dedicated to death and destruction.

The title "L'arca" ("The Ark") recalls the vessel that signified Liuba's frail hopes for survival, and in the case of this poem as well the metaphor stands for protection against parlous times. Far from "questa terra folgorata" ("this lightning-struck earth"; TLP, 245) where blood and quicklime boil, all the dead and gone of the narrator's past will gather again, shielded from the present horrors. Comforting and homey images embrace these souls, defending them, as it were, against the raging inhumanity of the here-and-now: a pot in the kitchen catches the reflections of their faces; and a magnolia tree in the garden drapes its boughs protectively over them.

In the poem "A mia madre" ("To My Mother") the lyrical speaker insists once more on the humanity and, paradoxically, the staying power of the dead. Even as "la lotta dei viventi" ("the struggle of the living"; TLP, 248) continues to storm, the narrator pleads with his departed mother not to surrender those features of hers that are so real: "*quelle* mani, *quel* volto, il gesto d'una / vita che non è un'altra ma se stessa" ("*those* hands, *that* face, the features of a / life that is itself, not another"; TLP, 248). This is the same theme seen in "Lungomare" and "Serenata indiana." The individual's form is shaken or blotted out, and one understands that the danger is that there will soon be no more individuals, only undifferentiated masses who have lost all human nature.

It may seem strange that the poet should choose the dead as beings on which to pin his hopes for the survival of the human personality, but this choice points to Montale's long-held affinity for the insubstantial and the meek. Clizia's powerful energies are truly exceptional for him, and they are continually outweighed in his verse by stories of weakness and fading.

On the positive side of the balance sheet of imagery in "Finisterre" are the jewels that Clizia wears: a jade bracelet in "La frangia dei capelli"; her hand, decorated with silk and gems in "Il tuo volo" ("Your flight"); or the coral earrings of "Gli orecchini." Indeed this type of "senhal" appeared in "Palio," where the woman gazed into a ruby, and will be found again in a sapphire and an amethyst mentioned in poems of the section "Silvae." It is easy enough to fathom the basic significance of these stones. They are standard figures for something precious, bright, and enduring. In "Gli orecchini," however, Montale uses them for more than their common value, inserting the emblems into a vignette. At the close of the poem one sees "squallide mani" ("squalid hands"; TLP, 239) grasp the coral earrings. In the context of "Finisterre" these hands can readily be understood as hostile, antithetical to the woman, though there is a more precise interpretation available, one that leads to a general problem in the analysis of Montale's verse of the 1930s and 1940s. In response to a critical skirmish over this passage, Montale wrote that the scene may conjure up the despoiling of the corpses of gassed Jews in the concentration camps—or may simply signify hands (evil hands, one assumes) reaching out of the darkness.[5]

In his published comments on "Finisterre" the poet several times asks that two levels of meaning be maintained in interpreting his allusions. Thus he says that "La bufera" treats the particular war provoked by a particular dictatorship—but also a "cosmic, perpetual war, involving all humans."[6] And à propos of another piece in the series, he comments that the references to the war are not to be taken too literally, but rather should be interpreted in "metaphysical" terms, as the doings of what are commonly called the "forces of evil."[7] Even more obviously than in *Le occasioni*, the poet here finds himself divided, pulled toward the vortex of the present moment, but also striving to stand back from that chasm and remain on the plane of what he sees as eternal questions. Likewise, readers are asked to suspend themselves between two possibilities: for instance, the specter of the German who wrenches earrings from a Jewish victim, and, on the other hand, the vision of a wickedness that has forever tested the good. No doubt such ambiguity will not appeal to everyone, and may indeed seem a strange position for someone like Montale who simultaneously stresses the importance of holding fast to the specific features of each human being, not letting the individual case be swallowed up in mass slaughter and general madness.

Two Interludes

Tilted definitely toward immediate events is the brief section "Dopo" ("Afterward") which follows "Finisterre." Two "Florentine Madrigals" make up half of this interlude. The first is headlined with the date 11 September 1943, leading one to expect a story of bitter disappointment. For in July of that year Mussolini had been deposed by his disgruntled lieutenants, and for more than a month

La bufera e altro 93

the war seemed practically over for Italy; the Allies, after all, had already taken the southern part of the peninsula. But on 8 September the Nazis intervened, establishing a puppet government in the North, initiating what was to be a reign of terror. Thus Montale's poem speaks of dreams that die aborning: hope, which had just revealed itself, must now be put away again, sealed up. And then a sinister, frightening note: an obscene graffito referring to Hitler is covered over with whitewash. Nazism is not dead, but springs to life again.

The second madrigal is dated 11 August 1944. The scene would make a startling news photo, a shot full of pathos: a dog gazes at the pylons of Florence's Trinity Bridge, sticking up like stumps in the middle of the river Arno. (In their retreat from the city, the Germans have blown up all the bridges except the Ponte Vecchio, the only one too narrow to accommodate tanks.) The war has finally ended for Florence, yet the poet immediately brings forth this unsettling idea:

> . . . s'infognano
> come topi di chiavica i padroni
> d'ieri (di sempre?)
>   (TLP, 252)

> . . . like sewer rats
> yesterday's captains (tomorrow's as well?)
> dive back into their gutters.

It is not that Nazism and Fascism—or the forces of evil—have simply evaporated. Rather, these "rats" have only scurried out of sight. And no doubt they could be quite adept at stealing back again, when the times are right. . . .

The longest piece of "Dopo" is entitled "Ballata scritta in una clinica" ("Ballad Written in a Clinic"), a poem in which private and public crises intersect. In the last days of the war, the poet and his companion, like Jonah carried in the belly of the whale, ride out days of terror. The woman (it is Mosca who appears here) has been stricken by a debilitating disease; the poet keeps watch at her bedside in a clinic. The momentous historical events are designated in the first line of the poem by the word "emergenza" ("emergency") with a small letter, but later the narrator also speaks of the *"altra* Emergenza" (*"other* Emergency"; TLP, 255), now with a capital E. This is an apocalypse of another order, situated on that plane of eternal, metaphysical disasters that Montale always returns to. But though the poet privileges the second crisis with a capital letter, he does not really disdain the anguish produced by the contingent, local emergency. Against the wanton violence of the war he sets a little barrier of personal effects that stand on the hospital night table: a bulldog carved of wood, an alarm clock whose phosphorescent hands give off a tiny glow. These objects serve roughly the same function as the flimsy guardian-emblems of Liuba or Dora Markus. They are, says the narrator, "il nulla che basta a chi vuole / forzare la porta stretta" ("the nothing which suffices for one who wishes / to burst through the strait gate"; TLP, 255). The "strait gate" is the Gospel term for the entrance to heaven and salvation, and Montale's use of the words is quite consistent with the spirit of the original, for he too sees merit in humility, mildness—signified in the ballad by the minuscule bedside trinkets that comfort the sick woman. In fact, the poet had earlier said that "L'iddio taurino non era / il nostro . . ." ("The bull-god was not / ours . . ."; TLP, 255), announcing with that metaphor as well his loathing for the violent and his allegiance to the timid. And at the end of the poem, with the arrival of a dawn that doubtless signals the long-awaited relief of peace, he looks out upon the multitudes of dead, then joins with the little carved dog in a mute wail of pity.

"Intermezzo," in contrast to "Dopo," is insulated from the emergencies of the moment. The first of this interlude's three pieces, "Due nel crepuscolo" ("Two in the Twilight"), as Montale informs the reader in a note, was retrieved from an old notebook and then revised. Almost twenty years after its composition, the poem resurfaces. This is an Arletta piece, suffused with the imprecise, shadowy idea of a woman, rather than a clear figure. One recognizes in the poem the metaphysical themes of the early Montale: the world seems to the narrator an unreal screen of images, and "not knowing" predominates over "knowing." The woman's visage and gestures appear to him strangely blurred and then, studying himself, the lyrical speaker finds his own movements oddly distant, alien. (One is reminded of the poem of *Ossi di seppia,* "Cigola la carrucola" ["The Winch Creaks"] with its vision of the narrator's dissociation.) So this encounter in the twilight is scarcely a meeting:

> Non so
> se ti conosco; so che mai diviso

> fui da te come in questo tardo
> ritorno.
>
> (TLP, 260)

I do not know
if I recognize you; I only know that I have never been
so divided from you as in this late
return.

The other two items of "Intermezzo" are prose pieces, foretastes of the narratives that the poet will begin to write regularly in the postwar years. Here he barely goes beyond the prose-poem, has not yet opted for extended efforts at story-telling. Thus "Dov'era il tennis . . ." ("Where the Tennis Court Was . . .") is loosely organized, revolving around a vanished place and time: Monterosso, and the poet's childhood summers. The tennis court overgrown with weeds is the emblem for this lost zone. The narrator also recalls an eccentric relative who tended cactuses and photographed them in bloom. A quixotic act, like any attempt to hold fast to a moment in the flow of time, and one rendered still more hopeless by the fact that cactus flowers are incredibly ephemeral things. Then, lastly, the poet's father emerges, with his quirky insistence even in August that the evenings are chill, quite chill. Indeed the cold was about to settle in, the narrator remarks, and the reader feels this change of climate as pregnant with meanings: the fading of childhood marvels, the death of an old order, and the arrival of a new age inimical to all the amiable eccentricities of a former time.

Disappearance and decline also figure in "Visita a Fadin" ("A Visit with Fadin"), the last part of "Intermezzo." In fact the poet Sergio Fadin, subject of this short commemoration, is destined to die, like Arletta, from a wasting disease. Yet instead of metaphysics or a "recherche du temps perdu," the prose piece dedicated to him turns to ethical questions. There is a lesson to be learned, Montale asserts, from this humble existence. The very lack of pretensions in this man Fadin makes him exemplary; there is a "decenza quotidiana" ("every-day decency"; TLP, 264) in his life that is identified as the most arduously attained of all virtues. To this admirable quality Montale adds another important trait: a will to "know" ("sapere")—even if one cannot hope to extract a stable, clear meaning from the welter of experience that the world offers.

The credo enunciated here is in keeping with Montale's long-standing hostility to any sort of dogma. He summons up the verb "sapere," so important in "Nuove stanze" as a token of resistance to mass folly. But he does not make of this "knowing" an "Open Sesame." There remains in his attitude some of the severe modesty found in "Non chiederci la parola," where the lyrical speaker offers no magical formulas. To exercise intelligence, to be aware, are moral obligations, Montale implies in "Visita a Fadin"—though only the arrogant claim to hold the meaning of the world.

In the note accompanying "Due nel crepuscolo," the poet suggested rather cryptically that he revised and published this long-lost piece because it still held an interest for him many years after its origin. Probably Montale refers not just to an antiquarian impulse in himself, a desire to reexamine his early writings. By inserting the Arletta piece into a triptych that also includes the ethical lessons of "Visita a Fadin" the poet in effect justifies his attachment to the "Twilight" mythology of weakness and fading. Neither Fadin nor Arletta is intended as an assertive character; their maladies assure that. But Montale finds in these apparently helpless victims a source of inspiration and conviction. In their very meekness lies their power for him.

The Fox Woman

The fox-woman ("la volpe") is the fancy that catches the poet's heart in the postwar years, the creature who shares the stage with Clizia in *La bufera*. The adventure with her is not a mere lighthearted foray, but the poems dedicated to this figure do depart from the grave manner of the Clizia pieces. Indeed Montale drew attention on more than one occasion to the differences between these two females in his portrait gallery. "Clizia and the fox-woman," he once commented, "are set in contrast, the first a savior-figure . . . the second a terrestrial being."[8] And in another explication, he specified that with the second cycle of Volpe poems in *La bufera,* the "Madrigali privati," an "Anti-Beatrice" enters his verse.[9] Indeed the transition from the heavenly Clizia to the earthly fox-woman may have been foretold in a poem from the sequence " 'Lampi' e dediche":

> ho amato il sole,
> il colore del miele, or chiedo il bruno,
> chiedo il fuoco che cova.
>
> (TLP, 271)

La bufera e altro 97

> I have loved the sun,
> the color of honey, and now I seek the dark,
> the fire that lurks deep.

Naturally one expects more than simply a change of "senhals" from this passage to the darker, earthbound figure. Like Clizia, the fox-woman will provide a vehicle for Montale the civic poet. Thus her poems continue the themes of elitism and hostility to organized religion developed under the sign of Clizia in *Le occasioni*. Most important of all, however, the Volpe cycle marks the beginning of Montale's polemics on the so-called "decadent" writers, a question which, as will be seen, is central to his postwar writing.

" 'Lampi' e dediche" and the "Madrigali privati" contain a series of references to God ("Dio" with a capital letter) that is novel for Montale, never one to pay homage to traditional religion. On closer inspection, however, the naming of God in the fox-woman's poems seems far from conventional piety. In fact in a poem of the "Madrigali privati," "Le processioni del 1949" ("The Processions of 1949"), one sees the woman in open combat with the traditionally religious. Pilgrims making a devotion to the Madonna are portrayed here in terms at least as unflattering as those found in the "Elegia di Pico Farnese." This religious exercise exudes "un tanfo acre che infetta / le zolle a noi devote" ("an acrid stench that infects / the ground vowed to us"; TLP, 311). And then the poet's angelic companion clashes outright with the pious:

> La tua virtù furiosamente angelica
> ha scacciato col guanto i madonnari
> pellegrini, Cibele e i Coribanti.
> (TLP, 311)

> your furiously angelic virtue
> has beaten away with a glove the pilgrims
> of the madonna, Cybele and the Corybantes.

The Virgin Mary is identified with Cybele, the Earth-Mother of antiquity, while her faithful are described as Corybantes, the priests of Cybele known for their noisy celebrations of the goddess. Obviously Montale makes this connection between Catholicism and pagan beliefs as a way of satirizing what for him is primitive superstition. (A similarly cynical view of the famous pilgrimages of postwar Italy may be found in several of Fellini's films; see especially the visitation of the Madonna portrayed as media event in *La dolce vita.*)

Equally indicative of an irony toward popular forms of religion is a vignette entitled "Vento sulla mezzaluna" ("Wind across the Crescent"). This piece is one of several travelogue poems in " 'Lampi' e dediche," reminiscent of the brief "occasions" of the 1930s. The scene is in Edinburgh, where, on one of the city's half-moon shaped streets, a preacher buttonholes the narrator, asking him if he knows "where God is." "Lo sapevo / e glielo dissi" ("I knew / and told him so"; TLP, 273) is the reply. But such an answer does not please. And in a kind of mock apocalypse (after the all-too-terrible apocalypses of the Clizia cycle) the preacher, along with houses and crowds, is caught up in a whirlwind.

Montale's narrator does not directly reveal his ideas as to God's whereabouts—it is the preacher who presumes to locate the Deity so precisely. But the first half of the poem has shown the lyrical speaker searching the city for the woman, and, given the precedent of the angelic Clizia, it will not seem farfetched if one suspects that the female figure here too represents a kind of divinity, furnishing the poet with his answer to the Great Question. Not that this woman partakes of Clizia's celestial qualities, however. For the lyrical speaker has said that he would be willing to pursue this lady "even navigating / through the sewers" ("anche navigando / nelle chiaviche"; TLP, 273), a perhaps disconcerting detail that nonetheless indicates her terrestrial nature.

Of interest for studying this nature is also "Incantesimo" ("Enchantment"), in which the narrator summons up the figure of Diotima, Socrates' mentor in love in the *Symposium.* The love-god that Diotima praises in Plato's dialog is a being "half-way between mortal and immortal," and serves as messenger between gods and men.[10] In less mythological terms, Diotima's speech describes the maturation of love as a process of being gradually weaned from attachments to terrestrial beauty and an arrival at the contemplation of absolute beauty, a bodiless idea. "Incantesimo" plays on this progress from a terrestrial to a spiritual love: the narrator speaks of the woman's "amore profano" ("profane love"; TLP, 281), and evokes images of heat and light—the flow of lava—that evidently signify physical passion; yet at the close, the poem points toward a future hour when the woman will lift the veil that has made her the promised bride of God. This image from the mystics' repertory is surely a vision of spiritual ecstasy, of the sort that Diotima set at the pinnacle of her curriculum of love.

It bears noting that the ideas of "Incantesimo" are analogous in a peculiar way to those of the Clizia poem "Iride" ("Iris")—which, perhaps not coincidentally, falls directly after "Incantesimo" in *La bufera*. Here again appears a dialectic between terrestrial and celestial, this time represented not by Diotima's love-god, but by the Christian heretic, the Nestorian, who conceives Christ as two beings, one earthly and the other divine. Clizia, of course, occupies the spiritual end of the scale; her presence in "Iride" is more ethereal than physical. And this is exactly what Montale has led us to expect in stating that Clizia stands in contrast to the terrestrial fox-woman.

The poet's commentaries on the earthly nature of Volpe could be illustrated with a number of poems. Among the most striking is "Nubi color magenta" ("Clouds the color of magenta"), where the woman becomes the courtesan Thaïs, while the narrator casts himself in the role of Paphnuce, the desert hermit. It is the tale of a pious man succumbing to the whore:

> Come Pafnuzio nel deserto, troppo
> volli vincerti, io vinto.
> Volo con te, resto con te; morire,
> vivere è un punto solo, un groppo tinto
> del tuo colore, caldo del respiro
> della caverna, fondo, appena udibile.
> (TLP, 312)

> Like Paphnuce in the desert, I desired
> too much to win you, but I was won.
> I soar with you, I linger with you; to die,
> to live becomes a single point, a knot stained
> with your color, hot with the breath
> from the cavern, deep, barely audible.

Seeking to convert the temptress to faith, the holy man is himself converted to lust. In the tumult of his passion, dying and living become the same—such is the delirium that Thaïs provokes. As elsewhere in her cycle, the fox-woman is linked to an earth sign, a cave. The heat and the heavy breathing, meanwhile, create a sensuous finale for the story.

This triumph of sensuality over spirituality gibes well with the earthliness of other Volpe poems. But the episode gains deeper significance when one situates it among the several references in the fox-woman's cycle to a cultural phenomenon, much studied by Italian critics, and known under the label "decadence." Oreste Macrì first pointed to the correlation between Montale's courtesan and the Thaïs portrayed in a novel by Anatole France (1844–1924), a writer linked to the decadent tendency.[11] Indeed France's *Thaïs* furnishes an exemplary text for studying the theme of the temptress, one of the stocks-in-trade of the decadents. The demonically seductive female has a special place in the repertory of "decadentismo," whether it is a Salome celebrated by the artists Gustave Moreau and Aubrey Beardsley, and by writers like Oscar Wilde and J. K. Huysmans (whose most famous book, *À rebours*, was translated into Italian by Montale's friend Camillo Sbarbaro), or the perverse and bewitching females created by D'Annunzio.[12]

Montale displays a penchant for the decadents during the early postwar years when the poems to Volpe are composed. Testimony to this attraction comes not only with the reference to France's *Thaïs*, but also in a piece entitled "Per un 'Omaggio a Rimbaud' " ("For a 'Homage to Rimbaud' "), and a citation, in the poem "Da un lago svizzero" ("From a Swiss Lake"), of the Baudelairian-Rimbaudian notion of "assassination." To comprehend Montale's interest in the decadents, here and later, it is necessary to review his impassioned postwar essays on the subject. For this artistic current which the poet judges innocent is under severe attack by Croce. And the question of "decadentismo" will haunt the last phase of Montale's work, putting to the test his convictions on art and politics and the way the two relate.

With the Liberation, the poet undertakes to defend those "modern" or "decadent" writers condemned en bloc by Croce as the bearers of a spiritual malady that both foreshadowed and abetted the rise of Fascism. In "Fascism and Literature" (1945) and "Does a 'Decadence' Exist in Italy?" (1946), Montale maintains that the decadents so loathed by Croce were actually innocuous. From the start, however, the poet's is a cautious homage. Rather than completely dismissing the Crocean accusations, he blunts them by asserting that the disreputable aspects of decadence have been balanced by benign elements. In "Fascism and Literature," for instance, he insists that "the cult of the irrational" and "theories of art construed as

La bufera e altro

pure magic, suggestion and allusion"—all that has been termed "decadentismo," in short—had little effect on Italian arts and letters.[13] Only refined and harmless versions of these decadent tendencies ever prospered in Italy, he claims. Contrary to what Croce argued, literature really provided no comfort to Fascism, with the exception of a few cases of crass collaborationism.

In his 1946 essay Montale formulates a similar apology, this time based on the distinction between "pure or alogical poetry" and a verse that, while suppressing as much as possible the "structural-rational cement" in favor of lyricism, nevertheless cannot be identified with pure lyric.[14] The first category, for the poet, includes works by Ungaretti and Rimbaud, while the second encompasses much of Hopkins, Valéry, and Eliot. In other words, Montale erects a cordon sanitaire around what he sees as the more dubious parts of "decadentismo" (which, as one will notice, has a broad definition for Italians, embracing many fin de siècle and modernist trends). The poet evidently identifies with the second of the factions he has named. Yet the boundaries he has established are not very secure. For he complains that many writers have been unfairly tried and executed by the "anti-decadents." Furthermore, he suggests that these two branches of modernism or decadence have much in common, and have been useful influences for each other.

It is striking that Contini, Montale's long time confidant in poetical matters, should have offered a rather different view of Rimbaud's connection to that branch of Italian modernism called hermeticism—and by implication, to Montale himself. In a 1940 issue of *Primato* Contini argued that of all the spiritual forefathers one might contemplate for hermeticism, none could be more appropriate than Rimbaud. Specifically, it is Rimbaud's attraction for altered states of consciousness, a reality not organized by traditional ideas of harmony and logic, that Contini saw continued in the hermetics.[15] But this Rimbaudian attitude is also close to Contini's descriptions of Montale as a poet who lacks "conviction in reality" and formulates a skewed world where "the irrational and the unexplainable" predominate.[16]

Montale cannot be pigeonholed as a hermetic, and indeed he represents a preexisting structure in the literary landscape by the time the edifices of hermetic theory and self-analysis are erected in the late 1930s. Nevertheless he is invited, evidently as an initiate, to comment on hermeticism in that same 1940 issue of *Primato*.

Here too the poet distances himself from the pure lyricism that he apparently saw the hermetics tending toward. Instead he insists on the "soul," which he predicts will inevitably return to poetry even when banished by a wave of writers dedicated to pure verse. The term "soul" ("anima"), taken from the vocabulary of idealism, may have a quaint ring in English translation, but Montale's meaning is clear: poetry as pure word- and image-play does not satisfy him; a message, an ethics must also be present.[17]

But the poet treads a thin line between irrational or even absurdist representations and, on the other hand, some rather traditional ideas of harmony, order, and meaning. The more cryptic "occasions" are nothing but modernist in their defiance of classical laws of exposition, and the poet's much-discussed "obscurity" attests to what extent his verse cuts away that connective tissue of rational structure alluded to in "Does a 'Decadence' Exist in Italy?" A definition of poetry that Montale was attached to in the postwar years also indicates the precariousness of his position between "irrationality" and conventional order. It is a comment attributed to the baroque poet and Jesuit Tommaso Ceva, according to whom poetry is a "dream in the presence of reason."[18] This seems to be Montale's program for art: a synthesis of the irrational world of dreams and the rationality of waking hours.

To Italian writers and critics of Montale's generation, the question of modernism's "irrationality" was a burning issue. One can understand the urgency of the question only by remembering the immense intellectual and moral influence of Benedetto Croce's diatribes against "decadentismo." From the beginning of the century, Croce had taken a jaundiced view of the decadents (again one must recall that the critic lumped under this label a broad collection of modernist currents), detecting in them a dangerous trend toward the "irrational," and predicting dire consequences if such a "spirit" were allowed to prevail. This analysis of "decadentismo" was repeated in the critic's histories of modern Italy and Europe, published in 1928 and 1932. The experience of Fascism—and, no doubt, the connections between the movement and such writers as D'Annunzio, Pirandello, and Ungaretti—furnished Croce with confirmation of his thinking, and so it is that in a polemic of 1947 he returns to denounce a wide swath of "modern" or "decadent" writers, held responsible for the "bestiality" of World War II. The unprecedented savagery of Fascism and Nazism, for the critic, was merely the complement of a "fragmented, unbalanced, disordered, inhuman soul" which the decadents had cultivated; irrationality in art ran parallel to irrationality in politics. Thus Croce turns with bitter and withering criticism against hermeticism and pure poetry, against Mallarmé, Valéry, and D'Annunzio—though perhaps his harshest attack falls on Rimbaud, judged noxious both as poetical and as moral example.[19]

Composing his poetic homage to Rimbaud in 1950, Montale maneuvers with the same delicacy as in his essays. He neither embraces this celebrated incarnation of modernism's disorder, nor allies himself with Croce's vilification of the "irrational" decadents. "Per un 'Omaggio a Rimbaud' " is a Volpe poem, and considering the scenes of frenzied passion the woman plays in other pieces, it is easy to understand how Montale can associate her with the enfant terrible Arthur. Yet having made this connection, the narrator raises his voice to beg the woman not to follow the too hectic course of the French prodigy:

> oh non seguirlo nel suo rapinoso
> volo di starna, non lasciar cadere
> piume stroncate, foglie di gardenia
> sul nero ghiaccio dell'asfalto!
>
> (TLP, 280)
>
> oh, do not follow him in his careening
> partridge's flight, do not let
> torn feathers, petals of gardenia fall
> on the black ice of the asphalt!

In this plea one hears the echo of Montale's calls for the extrication of a benign modernism from the more "irrational" strains of the tendency. The violence of the partridge's flight (and indeed the bird flies with a furious beating of wings) is to be refused, just as the "alogical" Ungaretti and Rimbaud are to be distinguished from the benign moderns.

Like "Incantesimo," the "homage" hovers between terrestrial and ethereal, for the narrator asks the woman, identified with a marvelous butterfly, to soar upward—apparently rising above the partridge's mad careening. He also calls her "daughter of the sun" and the phrase, adapted from Rimbaud's *Vagabonds,* seems not to signify the willful derangement of the senses practiced by the French poet.

Instead, Montale's use of the image suggests an ascent to the spiritual, the same kind of progress referred to in his mention of Diotima.[20]

Other pieces in the Volpe cycle also make use of the tradition of "decadentismo." For instance, the opening of "Da un lago svizzero" runs "Mia volpe, un giorno fui anch'io il 'poeta / assassinato' " ("My fox, I too one day was the 'assassinated poet' "; TLP, 314). This peculiar use of the word "assassination" has a complicated history, one that connects it to central parts of the poetics of Baudelaire and Rimbaud, and "decadentismo" as Italian critics define it. The standard etymology of the word, of which one finds a famous trace in Marco Polo, derives "assassin" from "hashish." In an eastern country, according to the tale told in the Venetian's travelogue, a tyrant maintained a corps of assassins by quartering them before and after their bloody deeds in a paradisiacal garden where the drug—their reward and tranquillizer—was always available. This legend finds a distant echo in Baudelaire's *Artificial Paradise* (1860). The French poet is not interested in an adventure story, however. Exalted states of mind are his concern, and he seeks to unravel the esthetic possibilities and moral consequences of drug-induced privileged moments. The other inheritor of the etymology, Rimbaud, has fewer qualms about such exalted states. He takes the excitation of the senses as a program to be fervently pursued. His prose-poem "Morning of Drunkenness" is written in praise of this kind of "assassination." "We have faith in the poison," he proclaims, asserting the disruption of normal states as a credo. And he concludes by hailing the triumph of his "method": "The age of the ASSASSINS is at hand!"[21]

Montale adopts the Baudelairian / Rimbaudian notion of "assassination" in much the same spirit that he deals with other aspects of the decadent tradition in his postwar writings. He will not liquidate the themes of "decadentismo," despite Croce's violent criticism. Assuming the identity of the "poeta assassinato," Montale's narrator flirts with the decadent exaltation of the senses, and enjoys a glorious sort of agitation. He is dazzled by the woman's image, setting off in feverish pursuit of her along a "solco pulsante" and a "pista arroventata" ("throbbing trail" and "scorching track"; TLP, 314). As these terms suggest, the chase is not cool or rational; the poet lives his delirium—his "assassination."

Indeed the Volpe poems often speak of the narrator's exhilaration and even frenzy, a state in which the reader is not accustomed to seeing the lethargic Arsenio. In "Luce d'inverno" ("Winter Light") every thought of the woman assails the poet with a violence and an electricity that exalts him; the spark that flies from his contemplation of her leaves him "nuovo e incenerito" ("renewed and burnt to ash"; TLP, 279). In the first of the "Madrigali privati" a ray of light from the woman promises to convert, as the narrator says, "my swallow into a falcon" ("perché se tu sciogli / quel buio la mia rondine sia il falco" TLP, 307). The metamorphosis is extraordinary, given Montale's usual affinity for the unassuming and mild; in *Satura*, after all, he will talk of the impossibility of changing himself from mouse to eagle, from timid creature to daring one. But the fox-woman has inspired him, endowing him with some of her own Dionysian spirit. In the poem "Siria" ("Syria") the poet tells of having found his voice again through her, and this reference to his own artistic potency certainly strikes one as a departure from the humility of the early Montale, so antagonistic to any lyrical abandon of the D'Annunzian sort. "Fascism and Literature," interestingly enough, had denied not only the influence of decadent "irrationality" in Italy, but also the exaggeration of the artist's ego.[22] Dangerous, in the Crocean analysis, were notions of the artist as titan (and hadn't D'Annunzio's artist-as-Superman blended into another cult of personality?). Yet in the Volpe poems, Montale reaches moments of self-celebration, and speaks of his poetic powers, not feebleness.

In short, Montale's reconsideration of "decadentismo" in the fox-woman's cycle also reaches into the much-discussed matter of his elitism. Croce had pointed accusingly at the decadents as irresponsible individualists, aristocrats with no concern for the common good. Attached to their art, they set themselves above the common folk for that reason, and the result was, in the critic's view, a sinister haughtiness.[23]

Montale's postwar essays betray his concern about these Crocean charges. To defuse them he defends, in "Fascism and Literature," the autonomy of the artist, his natural distance from any kind of partisanship. Then, in "Does a 'Decadence' Exist in Italy?" he rejects the Crocean call for the artist's engagement and emphasizes the "asocialità" ("asocial nature") of Italian writers.[24] Thus it is no surprise that in the contemporary Volpe poems Montale should hammer at the theme of the lyrical speaker's isolation from the many. The very title "Madrigali privati" suggests a refusal of public discourse. But even in a piece of " 'Lampi' e dediche," "Dal treno"

("From the Train") a "senhal" of the woman flashes, as the narrator says, "per me solo" ("for me alone"; TLP, 277)—indicating his separation from others. This phrase seems practically a leitmotiv in the fox-woman's cycle. In "Per album" ("For an Album") the situation is the same: the lyrical speaker detects signs of his beloved, and they are again "per me solo" (TLP, 313). And the piece "Se t'hanno assomigliato . . ." ("If they have compared you . . .") plays upon the metaphor used to great effect in *Le occasioni* and "Finisterre": the blindness of others. The sightless ones do not notice the angel wings that the fox-woman wears. Given this ignorance of theirs, the narrator can only ask, "con chi dividerò la mia scoperta, / dove seppellirò l'oro che porto?" ("with whom shall I share my discovery, / where shall I bury the gold I carry?"; TLP, 310). The culmination of this theme of aloofness comes in "Anniversario" ("Anniversary"), the last poem of the "Madrigali privati." The union between the fox-woman and her companion is construed in religious terms—he kneels, as though to worship her—but her beneficent grace will not be shared by others. As the narrator says,

> . . . il dono che sognavo
> non per me ma per tutti
> appartiene a me solo . . .
>
> (TLP, 315)
>
> . . . the gift that I dreamed
> not for myself but for everyone
> belongs to me alone . . .

Umberto Carpi has suggested that a specific political significance underlies this passage in "Anniversario."[25] Indeed the poem touches upon the war, recently ended, and thus re-enters the topical zone of "Finisterre." For Carpi, Montale's vision of divorce from others represents the poet's sense of malaise and frustration as the mass parties of postwar Italy, the Christian Democrats and the Communists, assert themselves. The poet had briefly been associated with the Action Party, which for a time offered the intelligentsia a middle course between the two ideological camps, but that possibility had soon dwindled and the nation was, by the late 1940s, basically partitioned into two monolithic factions. Carpi's interpretation is convincing and in effect gives a further rationale for Montale's adoption of so many of the decadent motifs relating to elitism and the artist's self-exaltation. The political motivations behind the poet's thinking will become even more unmistakable when one considers the contemporary set of Clizia poems and the "Provisional Conclusions" that close *La bufera*.

Dreams, Memories, and Postwar Politics

Croce was not the only voice damning the hermetics and decadents for their insulation from the world and their devotion to art. In an essay of 1941 that forecast with considerable accuracy the shift to realism in postwar Italian art, Giaime Pintor denounced, among other things, the school of critics that had grown up around the "metaphysical" Montale. Those who dealt with themes of "transcendence," or "religious conversion," those who detached themselves from the here-and-now to construct an "interior drama" are impatiently cast aside by the young writer. His generation, he says, has a completely real drama to enact.[26] Indeed Pintor was to prove himself a man of action, for he fell in partisan combat against the Fascists in 1943.

Montale delivered the text of "Fascism and Literature" as a radio address in March, 1945, and it is evident that he felt the artist's detachment and the transcendental vocation of art were in urgent need of defense. Italian literature, he maintained, had always been the "most indifferent to the contingencies of life, the least faithful interpreter of the times in which it was born."[27] And in that remove from the here-and-now lay, as far as the poet was concerned, safety: despite the designs of Fascism to nationalize culture, literature had remained essentially blameless and intact during the twenty years of the regime, true only to itself.

Montale's viewpoint did not prevail in the decade that followed the fall of Fascism. Instead, realism and immediacy, along with the political commitment of the artist, became the order of the day. Salvatore Quasimodo, for instance, a poet associated with the hermetics during the 1930s, converted after 1945 to an engagé stance. In distinct contrast to Montale's postwar essays, his "Discourse on Poetry" dismissed hermeticism and praised a new social and civic verse, poems that "answer or pose questions to me," the writing of the moment, of " '43, '44, '45 and of dates even closer to us."[28] Similarly, Elio Vittorini's influential postwar magazine *Il Politecnico*, though hospitable to Montale's poetry on occasion, nevertheless was basically intent on disposing of any idea of art for art's sake, and argued for an activist intelligentsia.

Antonio Gramsci, a founder of the Italian Communist Party and leading Marxist theorist of culture, did not live to see the postwar years, but his posthumously published prison notebooks joined these polemics of the late 1940s, offering a powerful critique of the perennially disengaged Italian artist. In *Literature and National Life,* Gramsci made special mention of Montale, accusing him of having slavishly "discovered" the Triestine novelist Svevo only after Svevo had been admired in Parisian literary circles. Gramsci's information may have been wrong (as Montale claimed), but he was accurate enough in situating the poet in an Italian culture wary of immediate social questions, enamored of a Europeanized—not popular or indigenous—art.[29]

It is against the backdrop of these calls for realism and commitment that one must read both "Silvae," a sequence of Clizia poems, and the "Conclusioni provvisorie" that close *La bufera.* In these pages Montale reaffirms, on the one hand, his allegiance to the memories and dreams that represent the contrary of the here-and-now advocated by postwar realists. In some sense he still lives up to Contini's description, seeking comfort in the past or in an interior world. Yet on the other hand the poet continues to develop civic allegories in his verse, commenting particularly on his own isolation, now due no longer, as he sees it, to Fascism, but to postwar mass movements and new totalitarianisms.

In "Proda di Versilia" ("The Shore of Versilia"), the poet, on another beach, resuscitates scenes from a Ligurian childhood: a crotchety grandmother tending her zinnias, mosquito-filled nights, preparations for a feast of seafood. All about are "vite ancora umane / e gesti conoscibili" ("lives still human / and gestures recognizable"; TLP, 292); even droll sea creatures and mice seem comfortingly familiar presences. But there is a jarring end to this idyll. In the last lines of the poem an unsettling vista opens, a "mare / infinito, di creta e di mondiglia" ("infinite sea, of clay and rubbish"; TLP, 292). One thinks of the sketch "Dov'era il tennis . . ." with its excursion into the peaceable kingdom of the poet's childhood—a vision that dimmed as an ominous chill set in. In "Proda di Versilia," moreover, the long-lost Ligurian places and characters are—or were—"still human," a phrase identical to one found in the fifteenth motet, where "humanity" represented by Clizia is threatened by the terrible machine-age robots. The ugly panorama that unfolds at the end of this poem, however, seems a less specific enemy; the piece is occupied mostly with commemoration and elegy, not attack on a new order.

"Voce giunta con le folaghe" ("A Voice Arriving with the Coots") also harks back to the poet's early days, but in this case the very function of memory is under scrutiny. The ghost of the poet's father and the spirit and the spirit of Clizia are interlocutors in this drama, set against the backdrop of the shore. Though they are both disembodied, the two shades are not of like opinion. Clizia, as is frequently the case, stands for spirituality militant. She is faithful to her convictions, "remembers" in that sense. "Ho pensato per te," she says, "ho ricordato per tutti" ("I have pondered on your behalf, I have remembered on behalf of everyone"; TLP, 298). Furthermore, she finishes by admonishing the father's ghost, too querulously concerned with memories:

> Memoria
> non è peccato fin che giova. Dopo
> è letargo di talpe, abiezione
> che funghisce su sé . . .
>
> (TLP, 298)

> Memory
> is not sin while it gives sustenance. Afterward
> it is mole-like lethargy, abjection
> that grows moldy on itself.

Here is the central question of the poem: at what point do recollections become complacency, a useless wallowing in nostalgia? No doubt the issue is partly literary, for Montale will not have forgotten criticism of *Le occasioni*'s poems of memory, chided by some as trivial exercises. But there is also a political dimension to Clizia's commentary on remembering, since nostalgic re-evocations of the past are not a popular genre in the postwar climate of commitment. Quasimodo's essay, for instance, accorded respect to the verse of the moment, while brushing aside writing that did not address the immediate. Montale is more reserved in his judgment. His poem endorses no idle journeys into the past, yet also insists on the value of the sort of "memory" that Clizia bears—a fidelity to principles, one understands, no doubt to that "humanity" often linked to her figure.

Dreams as well as memories have a peculiar prominence in the last Clizia poems of *La bufera,* as one can see in "Iride" ("Iris") the very first poem of "Silvae." In a note appended to this piece Montale says that he "dreamed" it, then transcribed its text; he calls himself the "medium" rather than the "author" of the poem.[30] The language and images here are actually no more difficult to follow than in many parts of "Finisterre" or *Le occasioni.* But the poet's postwar glosses on "Iride" betray again a need to defend his cryptic, allusive forms against the demands for directness and immediacy.

"Iride" also constitutes the culmination of the poet's idiosyncratic religious inventions. For the woman here has become a double of Christ. Her works, says the narrator, are a replication of His (". . . l'opera tua [che della Sua è una forma]"; TLP, 286). She represents, as Montale says in his own marginalia on the poem, the "continuer and symbol of the eternal Christian sacrifice. She pays the penalty on behalf of all, she suffers for everyone."[31] The signs of her presence reach the lyrical speaker through the "naufragio delle mie genti, delle tue . . ." ("shipwreck of my people, of yours . . ."; TLP, 285); the poet seems to invoke her to assuage the agonies of many.

The two peoples mentioned here are evidently Christians and Jews. Indeed the poem pointedly includes both Christian and Judaic imagery: a shroud that shows a bloodied, tortured face (probably the Shroud of Turin, reputed to be a kind of death-mask of Christ); and then the woman, who appears as "Iri of Canaan," a creature from the ancient Hebrew homeland. "Iride" thus continues the system of references to Jewish heritage found in the poems to Liuba, Dora Markus, and Clizia in *Le occasioni.* In effect this poem of the early 1940s joins the Christian and the Judaic—a merging that was perhaps suggested in the eighth motet. The meaning of this union scarcely requires explanation. Jews and Christians had been segregated in the most savage way by the Nazis and Fascists; Montale's poem sets the two peoples and traditions side by side, just as the motet spoke of a mingling of two bloods.

The narrator of "Iride," meanwhile, has called himself the "povero / Nestoriano smarrito" ("the poor / lost Nestorian"; TLP, 285). Montale provides his own commentary on the significance of this Christian heretic. The Nestorian, he says, is the "man who best understands the affinities that bind God to fleshly creatures"; neither to the spiritual, nor to the material will he give too much weight.[32] In "Iride" the Nestorian indeed hangs between the nightmarish present—he is driven into the boneyard, a place of slaughter—and beautiful visions, "senhals" of Clizia that stand for an exotic, faraway Palestine—"zaffiri celesti / e palmizi e cicogne su una zampa" ("celestial sapphires / and palm trees and storks standing on one leg"; TLP, 285). Doubtless this figure of the heretic presages as well Montale's convoluted postwar position on the place of art. The Nestorian seeks to mediate between transcendental impulses and the urgent appeal of the here-and-now. And while he confronts the present catastrophes of the flesh he never ceases to dream of the spirit.

The last appearances of Clizia in *La bufera* fall in the zone of transition from wartime to postwar years. The woman, who was carrier of the poet's political commentaries in the late 1930s, retains that role in his post-Fascist verse. Poems like "Iride" or "L'orto" ("The Orchard") show the woman as an agent of salvation, fending off the wartime terrors. In "L'orto" she comes down to earth as a messenger beloved of God. (Iris, too, in classical myth, was a messenger.) Like the seer-figure of "Nuove stanze" she faces with an unflinching gaze the horrible machinations of the warriors. While the poem of *Le occasioni* showed some disdain for the populace, represented by the image of the helplessly blinded pawns, "L'orto" takes a more charitable view. The war's Day of Wrath, says the poem's speaker, "Non ti divise, anima indivisa, / dal supplizio inumano . . ." ("did not divide you, undivided soul, / from the inhuman tortures . . ."; TLP, 290). The woman remains staunch, and does not insulate herself from the sufferings of others. (She is seen slaking the thirst of the dying and urging on those who still live.) "L'orto," similar to "Nuove stanze," tells of a vigil the poet keeps with the woman—he closes with an affirmation of their solidarity—but neither it nor "Iride" depreciates the multitudes engulfed in the war.

Most generous of all the Clizia poems is "La primavera hitleriana" ("Hitler's Springtime"). This piece was apparently long in crystallizing, for it is dated 1939–46. Indeed it embraces both apocalyptic scenes of war resembling those found in "Finisterre," and a taste of the joy and relief of the Liberation. The chilling inspiration of the poem is the meeting of Hitler and Mussolini at Florence in the late 1930s, during a state visit that helped seal the compact between

Nazism and Fascism. A "messo infernale" ("messenger of Hell,"; TLP, 295) flies down the Florentine streets, decked that day with hooked crosses—thus the demon arrives.

In Montale's account the Nazi-Fascist celebrations take on a tinge of the religious (hardly a surprise, given the poet's previous inclinations on the subject). Not only are the swastikas "hooked crosses," but incantatory chants ("alalà") and a "mystical" air accompany the ceremonies; these latter items, of course, summon up the quasi-religious rites devised by the Fascists to excite enthusiasm and awe in crowds. Frightening, too, is the way every innocuous festivity becomes an ominous portent. A toy store has . . . play guns in its window, while the butcher shop displaying a calf's head horribly signifies a human slaughter to come. The "sagra dei miti carnefici" ("festival of the gentle butchers"; TLP, 295) merges into a far less benign rite.

The narrator pronounces judgment: "più nessuno è incolpevole" ("no one is guiltless anymore"; TLP, 295). Even the seemingly innocent must share responsibility for the triumph of evil. The contrast between this line and "Nuove stanze" could not be more striking: no longer does Montale divide the guilt, leaving a few morally intact while the many become—even if only through witlessness—accomplices. Having distributed portions of culpability to all, however, the poem also offers redemption to everyone. Different religious motifs now enter the picture, counterbalancing the wicked creed of before. Clizia's signs are disclosed, including the sunflowers that Montale uses to represent his lady. And then the narrator beseeches her mercy, or rather her Christlike sacrifice for the sake of all:

> Guarda ancora
> in alto, Clizia, è la tua sorte, tu
> che il non mutato amor mutata serbi;
> fino a che il cieco sole che in te porti
> s'abbàcini nell'Altro e si distrugga
> in Lui, per tutti.
>
> (TLP, 296)

> Gaze a while longer
> toward heaven, Clizia; that is your destiny, you
> who, though changed, nourish an unchanging love,
> until the blind sun that you bear within you

is consumed in the Other, is destroyed in Him, on behalf of everyone.

Finally, the poet imagines "un'alba che domani per tutti / si riaffacci" ("a dawn that might reappear tomorrow, for everyone"; TLP, 296). Clizia's charity has been cast wide. In this poem at least the guilt is universal, and salvation is available to all. As in "Iride" and "L'orto," healing seems the first necessity in "La primavera hitleriana."

The season of reconciliation lasts only a short while in the Clizia poems. "L'ombra della magnolia" ("The Shadow of the Magnolia"), dated 1947, already finds the narrator bitterly reproaching others and showing the woman's faithful band as out of harmony with them. "Non è più / il tempo dell'unisono vocale . . ." ("Gone is / the time when voices were united . . ."; TLP, 300), he says, sounding almost wistful for those terrible days when moral choices were clearcut. Now they are more blurred, and when tested only a few citizens stand firm, watching as "gli altri arretrano e piegano" ("the others retreat, cave in"; TLP, 300). Autumn gloom, a metaphor used to political effect in Montale's verse of the late 1930s, serves here as well. The poet pictures a cicada in the magnolia tree, expiring as the seasons change, crumbling to dust. Its voice is stilled, a morose end for a piece that looked back almost nostalgically to the time when a chorus of voices sounded in unison.

Umberto Carpi has convincingly interpreted "L'ombra della magnolia" as an expression of Montale's political frustrations in the late 1940s.[33] Indeed the intelligentsia's moderately progressive Action Party would shortly disappear, pushed off the stage by the Christian Democrats and the Communists. To Montale, trusting ultimately only in government by an elite (an idea that, not very accurately, he felt Gobetti had championed) the postwar political arrangement in Italy could only seem a repulsive contest in which two sets of equally illiberal politicians cynically manipulated the multitudes.[34] No wonder that the poet should again talk in deprecating terms of "others"; in the postwar years, as in the 1930s, he sees himself in a tiny company of those who maintain their individuality and particular identity.

"L'ombra della magnolia" stands on the border between Clizia and Volpe themes. In fact the poems to the fox-woman develop with a vengeance the ideas of the narrator's isolation and the unworthiness of the crowd. (Carpi thus can extend his political analysis to " 'Lampi' e dediche" and the "Madrigali privati.") The last piece in "Silvae" also lies at a point of intersection between the two sets of inspiration. "L'anguilla" ("The Eel") sings a passionate ode to the beloved—doubtless this incarnation of the woman as eel is one of the oddest metamorphoses worked by a lyric poet in praise of his love—and makes one think of the fox-woman's frenzies and energy. In a delirium of naming, the narrator addresses the creature as "torcia, frustra, freccia d'Amore" ("torch, whip, arrow of Love"), then speaks of her revitalizing powers—new life springs up in the desolate places where she penetrates. The theme is quite close to that of the Volpe cycle: an earthly, animal-spirit rejuvenates and excites the lyrical speaker.

With the "Provisional Conclusions" Montale returns to overtly political themes, though there abides in these two pieces a tension between the poet's concern for the immediate and his desire to cast the commentary as timeless. At its outset, for example, "Piccolo testamento" refers not very cryptically to the postwar political alignments in Italy. What the narrator takes as his guiding light, he says,

> non è lume di chiesa o d'officina
> che alimenti
> chierico rosso, o nero.
> (TLP, 319)
>
> is not the lamp of church or of factory
> that sustains
> the red cleric, or the black.

Montale tauntingly conflates the two opponent ideologies, for the "reds" as well as the "blacks" as rendered as "churchmen." The sense of this equation is clear, and much like the message of the 1939 Clizia poems: these are two equally contemptible and dangerous dogmas, "faiths" that the independent intelligence cannot accept. Instead, the speaker of "Piccolo testamento" is comforted by a tiny beacon, an "iris" (perhaps in the sense of "rainbow"—which, we should recall, is a symbol of God's covenant with the Hebrews in Genesis). But the Clizia sign does not grow strong in this poem; indeed its insubstantiality is emphasized. It is closer to the faint glimmers of Arletta than anything else. And no doubt the poet means to take a kind of pride in the fragility of the individual who despite all odds determines to resist the mass movements around him.

The "testament" defends both the haughtiness and the meekness that may appear to lie in the poet's isolation. As he says, "l'orgoglio / non era fuga, l'umiltà non era / vile" ("the pride / was not desertion, the humility was not / cowardly"; TLP, 320). His aloofness may have been read either as excessive pride, or alternatively, pathetic weakness. But "Piccolo testamento" firmly claims that it was not a "trahison," no despicable abandonment of responsibilities. Here Montale insists again that his is an outsider's stance, and implies that his refusal of an ostentatious commitment was anything but a lack of integrity.

The most spectacular enemies of "Piccolo testamento," however, are not the faintly ridiculous black and red clerics. For the poem paints a dark, hellish future when "un ombroso Lucifero" ("a shadowy Lucifer"; TLP, 319) will come to rest on the shores of the Thames, the Hudson, and the Seine. On these rivers are situated the capitals of Western culture, and for Carpi that observation suggests that Montale's awful vision is a Cold War polemic: Lucifer must stand for the specter of Communism, horrific for the bourgeois poet.[35] Indeed, if one may judge from Montale's postwar political pronouncements, Stalinism would seem the most likely candidate to inherit the devilish imagery that the poet invented in the 1930s to portray Fascism and Nazism.

But no very precise key is supplied for the allegorical Lucifer of "Piccolo testamento," just as in the other "Provisional Conclusion," "Il sogno del prigioniero" ("The Prisoner's Dream") no exact definition attaches to the regime that holds the poet hostage. In fact the narrator emphasizes the perennial, nonspecific nature of his imprisonment: "la purga dura da sempre, senza un perché" ("the purge has gone on forever, without rhyme or reason"; TLP, 321). It would be plausible to cite Stalin's notorious purges as Montale's inspiration here, but it is also possible to take seriously the poet's attempt to universalize his story. In his career he passes from biting portraits of Nazism and Fascism, to hostile references to the "red clerics," to a sardonic look at the Greece of the Colonels (ca. 1968). In the highly polarized politics of postwar Italy such transitions are ideological blasphemy, but at least one must acknowledge the consistency with which Montale contemptuously disregards the party lines that distinguish Communism from Fascism, Catholicism from Communism. No interpretation of totalitarianism as a phenomenon bridging Hitlerism and Stalinism circulated in postwar Italy. (Hannah Arendt's thinking had a much wider audience in America than in Western Europe.) But one cannot deny that Croce and other spokesmen of the liberal intelligentsia—Montale included—were persistent in connecting and condemning Fascist and Communist practice. And such views, one can safely say, inform the poet's postwar verse.

"Il sogno del prigioniero" recapitulates some of the poet's familiar imagery: the "iris" appears again, together with a dream-vision of the woman. As in "Piccolo testamento," there are no angelic visitations or bright manifestations of good. There is, however, a grotesquerie that, as P. V. Mengaldo has noted, foreshadows the serio-comic language of Montale's satiric last phase.[36] The purge is a "sterminio d'oche" ("extermination of geese"; TLP, 321) and in the torture chambers of totalitarianism one can only choose whether to end up in the paté, or sell others to the meat grinder. The horrible metaphor cannot fail to summon up the hideous games played with human beings in the Nazi death camps. Montale, writing in 1954, chooses the worst hypothesis about mankind: that such inhuman sport was not an aberration, civilization's momentary lapse, but rather part of a pattern of purges that "have gone on forever."

Chapter Five
Satura and Afterward

"Botta e risposta"

Scattered through *Satura* are the three parts of a series entitled "Botta e risposta" ("Thrust and Parry"). The first piece in the group, coming directly after the dedicatory poem, serves as a gateway into Montale's last phase. It is an ambitious enough composition, for it gives nothing less than an account of the poet's times, from the "Augean stables" of Fascism to a postwar world portrayed as almost equally filthy. As even this brief resume suggests, the poem's outlook approximates that of "Provisional Conclusions," with its none-too-optimistic version of the world's fate after the regime.

The "thrust" of the first part takes the form of a poetic epistle from Asolo, in the Venetian countryside. Montale has underlined the significance of this place name and the reference to the Swiss spa Ascona in "Botta e risposta II." These two cities, he says, "are two almost inevitable points of reference for decadence: Ascona was a capital for homosexual intellectuals and early nudists of the late nineteenth century; Asolo, less sin-ridden, was however the favorite resort of romantics and the refined: Robert Browning journeyed there more than once."[1] "Decadence" is the key word in this comment, for the term calls up again those fierce polemics on this subject that the poet engaged in during the late 1940s. (Nor have the disputes cooled with time: an essay of 1962 finds Montale still contesting Croce's hostility toward the "detested decadents.")[2]

In fact, the very structure of "Botta e risposta I" indicates its function as a duel with critics. Thrust and parry amount to accusation and denial—though it is well to remember that the poet himself stands behind the mask of both the prosecutor and the defendant. Nor is it surprising that the first charge raised by the correspondent from Asolo should be that the poet has lived for too long in a state of suspension or detachment from his world. This was the original Crocean charge against the moderns, all too absorbed in their art, according to him. And just as in the late 1940s

Montale defended the artist's right to be "asocial," so here he continues to maintain the necessity of such an insulation from the here-and-now. Moreover, this defense of the artist's remove from the present is not simply generic. For the letter from Asolo begins by addressing "Arsenio," and that name from *Ossi di seppia* suggests that a very personal critique is being mounted, and that the poet is being called to account for a stance long implicit in his own verse.

Another theme from antidecadent polemics emerges in the second part of the epistle, though perhaps this issue is only a subtopic of the general question of the decadents' abstraction from the world. "Vivere di memorie non posso più" ("I can no longer live on memories"; TLP, 326) complains the interlocutor. The poet's defensiveness about "memory" had played a part in the poem of *La bufera*, "Voce giunta con le folaghe," and now it surfaces once more. To grasp the bitterness of this question, one can refer to a scathing postwar attack on the decadents' penchant for savoring things past. No doubt taking inspiration from Croce, the critic Francesco Flora claimed that this decadent fascination for memories testified to a "diminished sense of civilization" and a descent to barbarousness; abandoning mankind's collective memory, history, the selfish and contemptible decadents dwelt instead in private worlds of recollection, isolating themselves from the human community.[3]

The parry to the importunate letter from Asolo takes the form of a personal history wrapped inside a public history. Montale's justification of the artist's remove from his times, paradoxically enough, proceeds through a commentary on those times. The account of Fascism and post-Fascism offered in the riposte, however, is not of the type found in history books. Rather, the poet's retelling is allegorical, relying on the figure of the Augean stables. In this retrospective on his age, Montale continues to use a covert way of speaking, a stratagem not too different from the cryptic mode adopted in his verse of the 1930s and early 1940s.

Undeniably the poet is responding in a complex way to criticism of the decadent artist as one who absents himself from the real and present world. The narrator of "Botta e risposta I" will not plunge into public affairs at his correspondent's request; yet neither does he picture himself hidden away in some Asolo, without the slightest concern for the upheavals of his time. The formal correlative for this ambivalence toward *engagement* is the allegorical mode. Allegory both refers to a thing and is *not* that thing. Montale's account of

Fascism as the Augean stables both enters the here-and-now and refuses to enter the here-and-now:

> Uscito appena dall'adolescenza
> per metà della vita fui gettato
> nelle stalle d'Augia.
> . . . nei corridoi, sempre più folti
> di letame, si camminava male
> e il respiro mancava; ma vi crescevano
> di giorno in giorno i muggiti umani.
>
> (TLP, 327)
>
> Just past adolescence
> I was thrown for half of my life
> into the Augean stables.
> . . . in the halls, the manure piled up
> deeper and deeper, it was hard to walk
> and breathing was difficult; meanwhile day by day
> the bellowing of human beings grew louder.

The poet bitterly attests to his "involvement" in his times. How could one have escaped the monstrous filth of Fascism? he seems to ask. Were these modern-day Augean stables some minor blot, readily ignored?

The riposte also counters the interlocutor's weariness with memories. The critics of "decadentismo" might have charged memory with being irresponsible escapism, but in "Botta e risposta I" the narrator presents the mementos that he gathered during the Fascist period not as a flight from reality, but as necessary sustenance in difficult times. Such memories were not self-indulgence, he implies, but reminders of a dimension beyond the scarcely tolerable present. And as he conjures up souvenirs of Gerti, Liuba, and Clizia, one remembers the fortitude and sometimes the outright resistance to the regime that these figures betokened in *Le occasioni* and *La bufera*.

But no doubt the most controversial portion of "Botta e risposta I" is its depiction of the Liberation. For the stables of excrement that were the regime do not give way, in the poet's sketch, to a clean new world, but to another maelstrom of filth. Nor does a renewed nation rise up after the fall of Fascism but only a not-quite-human crop of "formiconi"—ant-creatures.

Actually, that Montale should portray Fascism and its aftermath as almost equally dismaying is not so surprising if one looks back to his reasoning on "decadentismo" and its enemies. For the poet saw the decadents besieged on all sides, not only by Croce's demands for a civic poetry, but also by the Fascist regime, and then, in the postwar years, by the Left. So it is that in "Fascism and Literature" Montale had rather maliciously linked Mussolini and the anti-Fascist Croce as would-be "dictators of poetry," bent on subjugating free-spirited artists such as the decadents.[4] Likewise, in "Does a 'Decadence' Exist in Italy?" the poet lamented both Crocean and Marxist assaults on the decadents, while in an article of the early 1950s he drew a comparison between Croce and Gramsci, both of whom are accused of unfair critiques of "decadentismo."[5] Constant in these many apologies for the decadents is a disregard for political distinctions. While others would see vast gulfs between Fascism, Croce's liberal politics, and the Left, what matters for the poet is that they are all equally hostile to that branch of culture with which he empathizes. (Of course this assimilation of widely different political groups into one uniformly unacceptable antagonist was already visible in "Piccolo testamento" with its red and black clerics.) The chief heresy of "Botta e risposta I," the continuity it sees between Fascism and the postwar epoch, is really just one more version of a concept that Montale's sympathies for "decadentismo" had already led him to formulate many times.

Having expressed his animosity toward both the regime and postwar society, the narrator of "Botta e risposta I" nevertheless allows himself little glory for his independent position. He does not depict himself as the Hercules who cleaned the Augean stables, and at the close of the poem he represents himself as a distinctly unheroic creature, not an "eagle," but a "mouse." One recognizes this self-deprecation as characteristic of Montale, for it was the poet's trademark from the time of *Ossi di seppia,* where Arsenio, for example, showed his weak and indecisive colors. It is also worth recalling that in Croce's analyses the decadents are elitists who eventually come to be possessed by a mania for power—consider D'Annunzio with his influence on the Fascist cult of the exceptional man. By way of contrast, Montale refuses the image of the artist as potent and grand: he proclaims himself not a mighty bird of prey, but a timid little creature. Yet at the same time this self-belittlement has not prevented the poet from turning to the multitude and depreciating them as "ant-creatures." Whether during the regime or after, the poet almost always presents himself as an isolated dissident surrounded by a contemptible collectivity. Perhaps the terms change somewhat; no longer is the object of scorn the Machine-Age men inspired by Fascism's enthusiasm for industrialization. Most likely the ants of "Botta e risposta I" (an archetypical figure for a dreary crowd) are tokens for the "collective life" that, according to "Does a 'Decadence' Exist in Italy?" was being propounded by the strenuously *engagé* postwar leftists as the most fitting subject for future art.[6] In defending the decadents and their quiet devotion to memories, the aged Arsenio makes clear that such an idea appeals to him not at all.

Though it does not rely on the political allegory of the first part of the triptych, "Botta e risposta II" also offers an apology for "decadentismo." At issue, beginning with the first line of the piece, is the poet's "solipsism." Solipsistic indeed are the denizens of Ascona, high priests of culture who isolated themselves in this "northern Capri" to celebrate in haughty solitude the rites of their art. The correspondent from Ascona wonders whether the poet was guilty of such solipsism. And, à propos of this charge, one cannot help recalling that in his essay on *La bufera* Contini spoke of Montale's "solipsistic imagination"—not with any accusatory intent, but merely to define a sensibility that dwelt more often on its isolation than its community with others.[7]

The asocial nature of the decadents has been taken to task again, but in "Botta e risposta II" the charge seems to be dealt with more lightly. Thus, at the start of his riposte, the poet summons up a whimsical version of his "solipsistic" past. Contemplating an ant crossing a brick pavement, he abruptly shifts perspective and says "Sto curvo su slabbrature e crepe del terreno / entomologo-ecologo di me stesso" ("I am bent over the crannies and cracks of the entomological-ecological terrain of myself"; TLP, 400). Just as "Botta e risposta I" exploited the name Arsenio as a way of acknowledging that an indictment of the poet's past poetic career was under way, so here another famous item from *Ossi di seppia* is resuscitated: the arid, cracked landscape traversed by ants in "Meriggiare pallido e assorto." This famous poem is evidently recalled as an ironic bow to those who would interpret Montale as the consummate solipsist, engrossed in trivial and arcane exercises of introspection, poring over a minute landscape and then arriving at a woebegone moral about the pain and sorrow of existence. The parry of "Botta e risposta II" makes a conceptual pun of such accusations. Solipsism equals self-absorption, and so the poet pictures himself entranced in contemplation of the "terrain" of his own body.

In this mocking fashion the poet seems to claim the right to his solipsism. Furthermore, the epistle from Ascona finishes by asserting that something still "holds" in that decadent watering place, and the poet in his reply certainly does not contradict that idea. He remembers a trip he once made to the Swiss resort and his encounter there with an obscure musicologist who had dedicated much energy to examining the authenticity of Haydn's works. This octogenarian is another specimen in Montale's collection of odd characters, devoted to what a more committed age would surely find an absurd and useless hobby, but respected by the poet precisely for his bizarre pursuit and eccentric individuality. Then, having recalled this strange character, the narrator remarks with scarcely concealed disgust that nowadays "un formicaio / vale l'altro" ("one ant-hill / is the same as the next"; TLP, 400). Which is as much to say that the ant-creatures of "Botta e risposta I" have prevailed everywhere, and such genial eccentricity as was once the hallmark of Ascona is now a thing of the past, erased by a less human mass society.

After this defense of the spirit of Ascona, the poet feels obliged to defuse once again the charges against the decadents' overweening pride, their elitism which could appear dangerous. Of course the old musicologist constitutes one refutation of the idea that decadent aloofness conceals a will to power: that ancient scholar may be removed from the common crowd, but he is obviously quite harmless. Then Montale mentions the classical philosopher Porphyry and his notion that the souls of wise people, being superior, survive in some incorruptible form. This apotheosis of the intellectual is refused; the poet instead sees himself a sea creature imprisoned in its shell—hardly a soaring, magnificent being. Like the first poem of the series, "Botta e risposta II" reaffirms the artist's separation from his fellows—his "solipsism"—yet purposely refrains from drawing a figure of immodest proportions, a D'Annunzian Artist-as-Superman.

The last poem of "Botta e risposta," while addressing many of the questions found in its predecessors, is distinguished by the fact that its epistle arrives not from a decadent locale, but from a contemporary time zone: the Greece of the Colonels. Even so, the poet once more manages to have it both ways, for though this piece of 1968 exploits for its backdrop the events registered in the day's headlines, it also avoids entering the political fray in a direct fashion.

Oblique references summon up the military regime that toppled King Constantine: the clamorous happenings are described as a boiling pot, bubbling noxiously. Offering condolences to his distraught Greek correspondent, Montale sets forth no fiery call-to-arms, but speaks instead of a passive, almost invisible resistance that is his meek standard. Not even words of revolt will he suggest, but only "shadows" that lie "between the words." These are the insubstantial weapons that he opposes to the new regime and its persecutions. He calls such shadows "l'essenza della memoria" ("the essence of memory"; TLP, 416) and says that they will survive inasmuch as they exist outside of "history."

This is a line of reasoning that has great importance in Montale's last phase. The poet has long been vociferous in his rejection of dogmas, from Croceanism to leftism. Now he seizes the term "history" and attacks that as well, ridiculing all those who use the word as a shorthand way of speaking of their conviction in the orderliness, the rationality of human events, and the inevitable upward progress of mankind. As a line from the poem "Dialogo" ("Dialogue") has it, "La storia è un *marché aux puces,* non un sistema" ("History is a flea market, not a system"; TLP, 378). Instead of nicely organized epochs and historical movements, Montale proposes a history whose sum total is only a hodgepodge of trinkets and trash. All sorts of odds and ends and waste products in fact abound in the poet's later works, from the successive waves of undifferentiable filth in "Botta e risposta I" to the real garbage of the poem in *Diario del '71,* "Il trionfo della spazzatura" ("The Triumph of Trash"). Generally, this detritus signifies Montale's conviction that the universe is composed of things that don't fit, don't belong—aren't reducible to a system.

Thus the piece "La storia" ("History") in *Satura* argues against all conceptions of history as orderly. History is not a sequence of neat links in a chain, the poem advises. It goes neither forward, nor backward. After a list of negations like these, however, "La storia" shifts gears, and in its second part reveals a sort of pale optimism of the last resort that one also finds in "Botta e risposta III." For however monstrous its destructiveness, however wicked the regimes may be, there are always odd bits of humanity that escape the devastation. No glory attaches to these survivors, just as the poet endows his eccentrics in "Botta e risposta" with no heroic posture as they stand outside the common crowd. But as usual he takes an ironic look back at those who remain part of the herd:

these prisoners, he suggests, are just deluded enough to imagine themselves more free than the strange escapees.

Mosca and the Satire of All Systems

The most conspicuous structures of *Satura* are the two sets of "Xenia" poems, each containing fourteen items. They bear dates from 1964 to 1968 and are dedicated to Mosca ("Fly"), the nickname of the poet's wife Drusilla Tanzi, who died in 1963. The "caro piccolo insetto" ("dear little insect"; TLP, 331) seems a figure of much reduced dimensions after her extraordinary predecessors. The august angel Clizia moved in solemn spheres and spoke in the highest of moral tones; the earthly demiurge Volpe, though in some ways less exalted, was nonetheless capable of being "furiously angelic." In the wake of these angels, Mosca strikes one as a winged creature of a lesser sort. In the second poem of the sequence the narrator addresses her, saying "povero insetto che ali / avevi solo nella fantasia" ("poor insect who had wings / only in your imagination"; TLP, 332). In short, she cuts a pathetic figure. Like Clizia, she may appear in the guise of a flying creature, but only of the lowest order, and anyway her wings are more wished-for than effective.

Mosca thus enters Montale's verse in *Satura* as the emblem of a stunted world. Furthermore, many of her poems are associated with the poet's satiric vein, with its demolition or parodying of coherent world-views and rational systems. At this point it is worth mentioning the question of the book's title. For it has been argued that Montale adopts the word "satura" above all in the sense of "miscellany" and that the meaning "satire" is secondary.[8] Yet even when the term serves to characterize the form of the collection, "satura" retains a satiric inflection, since the central satire of *Satura* is precisely a mockery of the systematic and an assertion that all is miscellany.

The shape of the "Xenia" poems gives a first indication of the poet's proclivity for the miscellaneous rather than the systematic. The portrait of the woman is fashioned from fragments, some so ridiculously brief as to seem composed exactly for the sake of deriding the ideal of the long, well-articulated composition. Here is an extreme example:

> Ascoltare era il solo tuo modo di vedere.
> Il conto del telefono s'è ridotto a ben poco.
> (TLP, 339)

> Listening was your only way of seeing.
> The telephone bill has drastically shrunk.

Two lines, and the eulogy is done. Montale, incidentally, was quite aware that the length of poetic compositions had become an issue for the critics of modern verse.[9] To those nostalgic for traditional ideas of structure and development, the brief utterances of modern poets (Ungaretti comes to mind) seemed madly disjointed. With Mosca poems like this, Montale in effect makes sport of such traditional rules.

One also ought to note that the initial vision of Mosca in the "Xenia" poems (for she is a revenant here) appears to the poet as he is consulting "una bibbia sfasciata ed anche poco / attendibile" ("a tattered and not very reliable Bible"; TLP, 332). This detail may suggest that her return is correlated not with any faith in a comprehensive interpretation of life on earth, but rather with the doubt that any such world-view could be valid. Religion as a key to the universe is not an idea that informs the "Xenia" poems. Mosca indeed has a religion that is an improbable combination of petitions to St. Anthony for the recovery of lost umbrellas, and prayers for the dead—a haphazard repertory of superstitions which the priest at her death kindly accepts as "sufficient." Moreover, she has a special affinity for the eccentric and the unlikely, for "persone inverosimili" ("improbable characters"; TLP, 348). Explainable events and ordinary people do not exist in the "Xenia"-world, only the curious object (a rusty shoehorn somehow become precious over the years) and the bizarre type (a Mr. Cap, an Austrian lawyer peculiar for his name and perhaps much else). In line with this general disorder, Mosca's last moments are evoked not as the occasion for the summation of a destiny, but as a series of disconnected recollections—"nugae," or inconsequential items, as the poet calls them, using a word that Latin poets invoked in deprecating reference to their works. Mosca's parting is in the spirit of the deathbed witticism attributed to Gertrude Stein. Asked at the last minute for the "answer," Stein is reputed to have replied, "What was the question?" Likewise there is no final answer given at Mosca's expiration, because one could hardly formulate a comprehensive question about life, seeing that it is only a random medley of impressions and incidents.

Mosca frequently presides over the reduction to absurdity of circumstances and institutions that are supposed to command respect. At a testimonial dinner for the poet in Portugal, the modern equivalent of that solemn ancient ceremony on the Capitoline in which the bard was crowned with laurel, she is reduced to mirth. In her eyes the pomp turns to something vastly amusing:

> La sera fui paragonato ai massimi
> lusitani dai nomi impronunciabili
> e al Carducci in aggiunta.
> Per nulla impressionata io ti vedevo piangere
> dal ridere nascosta in una folla
> forse annoiata ma compunta.
> (TLP, 356)

> That evening I was compared to the Lusitanian
> Greats with their unpronounceable names
> and then even to Carducci.
> I saw you, not at all impressed, laughing
> till tears came, in a crowd
> perhaps bored but suitably reverent.

Mosca's skepticism on the occasion of this investiture gibes well with another meditation on poetry found in the "Xenia" cycle. Here she stands for a mistrust of the grandiose versions of poetry endorsed by the general opinion:

> Dicono che la poesia al suo culmine
> magnifica il Tutto in fuga,
> negano che la testuggine
> sia più veloce del fulmine.
> Tu sola sapevi che il moto
> non è diverso dalla stasi,
> che il vuoto è il pieno e il sereno
> è la più diffusa delle nubi.
> (TLP, 344)

> They say that poetry at its height
> magnifies the Whole in flight,
> they deny that the tortoise

> may be swifter than the lightning bolt.
> You alone knew that motion
> is no different from stasis,
> that emptiness is fullness and a clear sky
> the most diffuse form of cloudiness.

Doubt is cast on the notion of poetry as capturing some sort of Totality. Mosca serves as a mascot for skepticism in this matter; the conventional distinctions, the standard conceptualization and organization of experience are not for her.

The last piece in the "Xenia" poems is an especially melancholy picture of the world-in-confusion. Motivated by the 1966 flood that did immense damage to Florence's artistic wonders, the poem speaks of the disaster that befell the poet's own little store of cultural treasures: editions and mementos of Ezra Pound, Valéry, and Dino Campana (the list is something like Montale's idiosyncratic selection of Modern Greats). All these artifacts are destroyed when the basement housing them is inundated with mud and water. Then, using an image of filth similar to that of "Botta e risposta I," the poet portrays himself engulfed, like his books, in a dirty tide—beset, as he puts it, by "gli eventi / di una realtà incredibile e mai creduta" ("the events / of an unbelievable reality I never really believed in" TLP, 360). The world is past comprehension, the wanton depredations of history as unforeseeable and uncontainable as the Arno's destructive torrent.

The poems to Mosca are rarely hopeful. She does not have much in common with the courageous Clizia, confronting the war machine of Fascism, or Volpe, fount of exhilaration. Yet at the close of his account of the catastrophic flood, the poet does offer a brief homage to the woman, attributing to her the courage that allowed him to persist through all the disasters. Moreover, in a few other "Xenia" poems, the narrator does summon up the vanished figure with something akin to tenderness—recalling, for instance, her passion for telephone calls, or her poor eyesight, which made his guiding arm essential when there were stairs to descend.

Principally, however, she plays a destructive role. Arletta was a boy's fantasm, and Clizia and Volpe were mature love and passion, but Mosca represents the harridan, the fellow inmate in a prison of domestic miseries. She laughed uproariously at the poet's installation among the Portuguese bards; and indeed her laughter, as another poem has it, was like "l'anticipo di un tuo privato / Giudizio Universale, mai accaduto purtroppo" ("a foretaste of your private / Day of Judgment, which unfortunately never took place"; TLP, 341). *Diario del '71*, the work that follows *Satura*, gives the harshest proof of Mosca's cruel judgments. In "Il pirla" ("The Prick") the obscene epithet of the title is flung at the poet by the dying woman, and he can only wonder stoically if others in the world must also bear the stigma of this label, if they feel the need to somehow scratch it off.

As with the other female figures in Montale's portrait gallery, any account of Mosca will fluctuate between the private and the public. The verse dedicated to Clizia may be love poetry, but for an Italian Anti-Fascist, this woman also holds a special meaning in that she is American and Jewish. Similarly, the fox-woman is a heady liaison, yet also becomes the mouthpiece for postwar polemics. Mosca's harsh tongue, finally, is quite consonant with her role as presiding spirit for the poet's own sardonic demystifications. His exercises in deflation and *reductio ad absurdum* find their specific targets in two of his pet antipathies, the Crocean and the leftist world-views. These are the subjects attacked in two poems which Montale identified as pieces dedicated to Mosca.[10]

"Cielo e terra" ("Heaven and Earth"), the poet informed his commentators, is devoted to mocking the Crocean idealist version of history.[11] Satirized is the view that sees human events produced by the unfolding of "spirit," some transcendent quality that, in Croce's account, is also immanent in man. This sort of history contains a determinism that Montale will not accept. In fact he prefers to regard events as *not* advancing according to any scheme at all. The poem makes sport of the cleverly contrived circular process by which a transcendent "spirit" descends from above to guide the course of earthly events, even while man busies himself fashioning more transcendent "spirit" according to his time and place, his wants and needs, so that he may send it back up to heaven, so that it may descend again to guide him, and so forth. But, says the poet, "il cielo non è un boomerang / gettato per vedersi ritornare" ("heaven is not a boomerang / hurled only to see it return to oneself"; TLP, 408).

"Cielo e terra" is a late skirmish in Montale's long war with Croce. The previous battles had centered on the question of decadence, but there is a relationship between that literary dispute and the model of history ridiculed in this poem. Croce is the great champion of "synthesis," whether in his literary criticism or in his analyses of historical events. Modernist visions of breakdown and confusion—or modernism's preference for fragmentary, antitraditional forms—are subjected to withering attack by the critic. Likewise, in his histories, Croce demands "synthesis," which is to say a peaceful conciliation of antithetical forces, an orderly march forward in the name of progress. (Thus for him Fascism is a "parenthesis" of unreason, a brief interruption in the smooth evolution toward an ever-better civilization.) One scarcely needs to repeat that Montale is not in agreement with the critic's preference for classical forms and robust optimism in poetry. But in his 1962 essay on Croce, the poet also took issue with the philosopher's neo-Hegelianism, including its ordering principle, or "spirit," and, ultimately, its confidence "in seeing in history an infallible progress not from evil to good but from good to better."[12] Montale does not envision events unfolding according to any such idealist script, nor does he have the conviction in a steadily improving mankind that he detects in Croce.

Another poem of *Satura* identified by Montale as belonging to Mosca's domain is "Piove" ("It's Raining"), the title and form of which parody D'Annunzio's celebrated "La pioggia nel pineto" ("Rain in the Pine Grove"). Certainly there is a peculiar consistency in this return to the antagonist that had preoccupied the poet fifty years earlier in *Ossi di seppia*. And perhaps the deflation of the pretentious poets laureate in "I limoni" appears, in retrospect, as a not implausible ancestor for the satiric verse of half a century later.

But "Piove" is concerned not only with parodying D'Annunzio and the "favola bella" ("beautiful tale") of his verse. Also satirized are a host of modern concepts, or "epistemes," lumped together for wholesale deprecation much like the ideas of history stuffed into "La storia." Among the authors of these epistemological advances are the "teologi in tuta" ("theologians in coveralls"; TLP, 390), a reference to the left that again brings to mind the "red clerics" of "Piccolo testamento." As "Piove" makes clear, a system of belief centered on the concept of the working class convinces the poet no more than the Crocean vision of an always advancing humanity.

Satura's skepticism cuts a wide path, assaulting not just the most imposing and significant systems, but even the more individual attempts at making sense of human life. "A un gesuita moderno"

("To a Modern Jesuit"), for instance, takes Teilhard de Chardin to task for his peculiar theory of a "noosphere," represented by Montale in jocular terms as an atmospheric layer suffused with human spirit and enveloping the globe. As was apparent in his tale of the "poor lost Nestorian" in *La bufera,* the poet has his own idiosyncratic resolution of the contest between spirit and matter, transcendence and immanence. But he has little patience when others tinker at this philosophical puzzle. The Jesuit philosopher / anthropologist's "noosphere," Croce's neo-Hegelian "spirit," and the "uomo indiato" or the "cielo / ominizzato" (roughly, "divinified man" and "humanified heaven"; TLP, 390) of "Piove" are all targets for his barbs. Perhaps what Montale objects to most fundamentally in all these theories is the excessive optimism implicit in them. In his "Imaginary Interview" of 1946, he spoke of the mediation between "immanence" and "transcendence" attempted by such philosophers as Croce, and remarked that this perennial question was not, finally, to be resolved, and surely not resolved with a smug reconciliation of the two terms, with a "parade-ground optimism."[13]

More Thrusts and Parries: Pasolini and Montale

One of the more incisive critiques of *Satura* was presented by Pier Paolo Pasolini, who, accurately enough, saw Montale's satire directed against "positivism," "Hegelianism," "Marxism," and any notion of "progress." More polemically, Pasolini suggested that *Satura* was a hypocritical enterprise, since in spite of its demolition of all these systems, it also gave enough glimpses of the author comfortably ensconced in his bourgeois world and in his role as famous poet to indicate that his was only armchair nihilism. For all his sniping, Pasolini claimed, Montale still relied on the powers conferred by his class and by the traditional status of the artist in society. "Cowardice" was the review's final verdict on the poetry of *Satura.*[14]

Nor did the matter rest there. Only a few months after this review, Montale composed a poem called "Lettera a Malvolio" ("Letter to Malvolio") that Pasolini took as a rebuttal. The piece, eventually included in *Diario del '71,* presented the usual justification for the poet's aloofness from his surroundings, denying that it was a question of cowardly flight, and then turned with venom on Pasolini.

Indeed this novelist, poet, and filmmaker seems the ideal contrary for everything Montale believed in: a Marxist (albeit unorthodox) who had sworn off his decadent origins, a celebrator of the people, especially the lowest strata of society, an artist who had engaged a wide public with his controversial films, frequently containing religious motifs, yet also attacked by the censors as obscene. And perhaps one should also note that during the 1950s and 1960s Pasolini's writings had often invoked that portentous word "history"—not to deprecate it, but to acknowledge its power. Not surprisingly, Montale's view of this antagonist was harsh:

> Con quale agilità rimescolavi
> materialismo storico e pauperismo evangelico,
> pornografia e riscatto, nausea per l'odore
> di trifola, il denaro che ti giungeva.
> (TLP, 522)
>
> With what adroitness did you blend
> historical materialism and evangelical pauperism,
> pornography and redemption, nausea at the smell
> of truffles, the money that poured in.

Montale turns the charge of hypocrisy launched at him back toward its author, depicting Pasolini as cynically bent on gain—singing the praises of the poor while collecting fat royalties.

Although explicit enough about the alleged sins, the epistle to "Malvolio" did not explicitly name the sinner—a form of contempt Montale had also employed in his allusion to Mussolini in "Botta e risposta I." Thus when Pasolini replied to the poem he drew attention to that omission, referring to Montale's "all too obscure Italian Muse," and identifying the poet with a wickedly crafty Odysseus who pokes out the eye of the Cyclops but refuses to fight openly, getting off scot-free through use of the riddle-name "No one."[15] A clever response, but even more than that, Pasolini's epigrams of rejoinder sum up the bitterness with which a significant part of post-Fascist Italian culture had regarded hermeticism and its allies. The cryptic language of that generation was a sign, for many of those who came afterward, not of superior art, but of inferior humanity.

Angels and Miracles in *Satura*

Besides duelling with critics and satirizing systematic worldviews, Montale's late work also offers a final assortment of portraits-of-the-female. Of course there is the "Xenia" sequence that, even if it is mostly composed under the sign of shattering satire, nonetheless has a wholeness of inspiration close to that of the Clizia or Volpe cycles. But chiefly these are less concentrated efforts, odd visitations by "incognito divinities," as a title of a poem from *Satura* has it, or late reminiscences of figures from earlier days, above all Arletta and Clizia.

These poems often partake of Montale's relaxed later style. As he once remarked, his first three books were composed by a poet in formal dress, while from *Satura* onward one sees the writer in pajamas—or at least in more casual attire.[16] A good example of this informality comes in "L'angelo nero" ("The Black Angel"), a puckish piece, as whimsical as some of the verse dedicated to Mosca, but completely without their acidity. The angel of the title is not majestic, doesn't tower over vast celestial realms. This is a divinity in keeping with the scaled-down world of the later Montale, a "miniangelo" ("mini-angel"; TLP, 426). The prefix, drawn from slang popular in the 1960s and 1970s, is itself a deliberate thumbing-of-the-nose at the sublime. Furthermore, this elfin angel has a fugitive quality, like so many of the things in which the poet puts his faith, especially in his *Satura*-phase. Haunting kitchen fires and street vendors' braziers, the sooty urchin-divinity occupies peculiar, out-of-the-way spaces, something like the odd escapees from "history" in "La storia," or the shadowy tenets of conviction of "Botta e risposta III."[17] Yet the poet also calls this little angel "great." What seems insubstantial and insignificant metamorphosizes, as often in Montale, into the most important, even the miraculous. "O grande angelo nero" ("O great black angel"), says the poet, but also sighs "o piccolo angelo buio" ("o little dark angel"); and his very last invocation is:

>   . . . grande angelo
> di cenere e di fumo, miniangelo
> spazzacamino.
>   (TLP, 425–26)

> . . . great angel
> of ashes and soot, mini-angel
> chimney-sweep.

The longest suite of poems after the Mosca cycle is a group called "Dopo una Fuga" ("After a Flight"), eight pieces that amount to a discursive narration of the poet's passion for a fey young woman. Somehow he develops a special empathy for this woman who hurls objects out the window and threatens to jump after them. He seems to divine from her madness that she shares his miseries. His path led him "tra i demoni e gli dèi, indistinguibili" ("among demons and gods, indistinguishable"; TLP, 445), and later he adds that the woman's path as well must have taken her past hell. This "inferno," it should be noted, is not so much a place of Medieval terror as of modern day confusion and muddle. Devils and divinities cannot be separated, a Babel of voices sounds, sirens on the street numb the brain. These details constitute another of *Satura*'s depictions of the world as jumble. Thus it is as a fellow victim of a world-in-chaos that the poet singles out the woman and takes comfort from her. Moreover in describing her, he invokes the archetypical metaphor for the overly civilized world's escape from corruption: the noble savage. The American Indians fleeing from the white man would have welcomed the woman into their company, he says, suggesting in this way that she is as pure and authentic a spirit as they.

In the middle of "Dopo una fuga" the poet comments wryly on his reputation for agnosticism, for creating a universe of negation, from which he conjures up at the last minute a bit of hope: "Si dice ch'io non creda a nulla, se non ai miracoli" ("People say that I don't believe in anything, except miracles"; TLP, 446). Indeed one feels that the young woman could serve as a "miracle," taking her place beside other visitations of grace in the poet's verse. But nothing like the great, solemn myth of Clizia and her miracles is to be repeated in "Dopo una fuga." In fact, the poet deflates his tale even as it unfolds. He contemplates a parallel between himself and King Lear, and between the young woman and Cordelia. But that story is high tragedy, and "Dopo una fuga," one understands, is closer to farce. Mercilessly the poet represents his attraction for the woman as a foolish daydream—nothing to match the tempestuous folly of Lear which brings about a vast, resounding fall. Part of this farcical, rather than tragic, quality is wrought with the modern words Montale uses at this juncture: "Hovercraft" and "Hydrofoil" (in English in his text), conveyances he fancies he might adopt to steal the young woman away. With these "neologisms," as the poet terms them, the fantasy passes even beyond the improbable to the ludicrous. A bathetic note is sounded when the vehicle of the passionate lover is not a noble steed but a hydrofoil—just as when angels become "mini-angels."

The last piece in the sequence retrieves a little dignity for the poet, though at the price of his withdrawal from the adventure. He assumes, however, that the woman will consider her part done if she has provided him with inspiration. The emotion of the affair is embalmed in this way, yet there is also a wistfulness in this close, contained especially in the idea that these modern times which the poet has survived to see have managed to snuff out the old-fashioned dramas of passion. As he remarks parenthetically of his trauma: "ora nessuno sviene / per quisquilie del genere, il cuore a pezzi o simili" ("nowadays nobody faints / over such trivialities as these, broken hearts and the like"; TLP, 449).

Like much of the later Montale, "Dopo una fuga" is veined by the perception of the present day as base metal, not precious. Emotions have been devalued, the tragedy of Lear has been replaced by a rather pathetic story, modern times present a confusion of values and voices, and even the linguistic potpourri of the moment helps to signify bathos. The "miracle" of the woman tentatively pokes through all this debris—though the word is brought up in the course of a quotation ("People say . . ."), as if the poet did not quite believe the concept himself and needed the support of outside authorities.

Pieces of serendipity remain in the poem, and perhaps the strongest is the ninth part of the sequence, which, following Montale's stipulation, is not included in Italian versions of "Dopo una fuga." Swearing off the felicitous ending, the poet removed these final lines to America, where they were first published in English translation. And perhaps the implication is that, at least as far as the poet goes, some trace of innocence and potentiality still clings to the New World (after all, didn't the noble savage figure in these poems?) and the dream or miracle could be appropriately confided to that continent:

> Extraordinary your arms. When
> I die come to embrace me, but
> without your sweater.[18]

Last Returns of Clizia and Arletta

In the last years of his poetry, Montale brings back Clizia and Arletta on occasion, not for any ambitious re-creation of these figures and their motifs, but in a mood of mostly bemused reminiscence. Indeed it is fitting that the poet, having exploited "memory" for so long in his verse, and then having spent much energy defending the virtues of recollection, should finish his career with final journeys into the past.

In these pieces the poet seems to ask one more time the question that his doubt-filled, paralyzed alter ego began to pose in *Ossi di seppia:* what significance could these chance encounters, these female apparitions, hold? In "Quartetto" ("Quartet"), a yellowed, forty-year-old photograph showing Clizia, the poet, and others at Siena's Palio emerges from a drawer, and this souvenir (besides reviving the chill vision of a crazed crowd) demands an answer to the problem of how things can exist in time and space—and then exist no more. In another piece, "Interno / esterno" ("Interior / exterior"), a phone call out of nowhere, from an old friend of Clizia's, puts the same sort of metaphysical question to the poet. And, on a less esoteric level, there is also a political issue which surfaces in these latter days. (Appropriately enough, since Clizia, as a key element of Montale's Anti-Fascism, certainly played a political role in his verse.) The piece "Nel '38" ("In '38") records the report that Clizia harbored leftist sympathies. This news evidently does not sit well with the poet, yet in the end he appears to shrug it off as still another baffling aspect of that whimsically confused world he often portrays in *Satura* and afterward.

Despite all these late doubts, Clizia keeps a tinge of the miraculous about her. Thus it is that the poet can assert his belief in her once more, speaking of a "faith" that will endure until the two are reunited in a place beyond the "immenso cascame" ("immense rubbish-heap") of the present world.[19] Clizia as well has been set against the backdrop of muddle that predominates in Montale's final phase, though even so the poet does not renounce the conviction and power she represented for him in the past.

The last appearances of Arletta (also called Annetta) are not vexed by political questions, but they do provoke the same kind of metaphysical ruminations as Clizia's late returns. In the poem "Annetta" the girl's brief life and the poet's rare, strange reminiscences of her, sporadically surfacing over the many years, lead him to wonder about notions of reality and unreality. And, as in his earlier days, Montale here tends to privilege what seems "unreal" (fugitive figures like Arletta / Annetta) with a greater reality than the things that are commonly accepted as being real and solid—the here-and-now.

A special charm of this piece lies in its vivid evocation of a little theatrical performance that the poet and the girl once staged for the household. Here Montale is at his most Proustian, savoring a morsel of the past that suddenly yields all its flavor again. The careful, defensive justifications of "memory" seen in earlier verse are no longer brought forward in "Annetta"; the recollection appears and is unashamedly embraced as the most real of all things.

As Montale said in a late interview, Annetta remains the "most real character" in his work, the one that "endures through time."[20] Indeed the last item in the last collection that the poet issued is a piece called "Ah!," dedicated to Arletta / Annetta, the beginning sound of whose name the title seems to mimic. She has disappeared, and long ago, but the poet imagines her surviving in who knows what place, and perhaps reading his verse, trying to remember his face and the faces of others. In this last moment the poet again sets up his unreal, house-of-cards communion—and seems to ask whether this ethereal, imaginary communication isn't the most real of all.

Chapter Six
Conclusion

Montale's poetry has often been a battleground for different schools of interpretation. More than one critic has heatedly written to rebuke those who would dare read political dimensions in the poet's early verse, and others have been equally indignant about attempts at biographical criticism, convinced that all the information one needed to know about Arletta, Clizia, the fox-woman, and Mosca was already apparent in the works themselves. The life of these figures off the page, ran the argument, was not really of concern to those studying the poetry. On the other hand, analysts devoted to political exegeses of Montale have often denounced formalist critics as naive and superficial. Tracing the repetition of an image through the course of the poet's verse might be of some interest, but in the end how valuable could such studies be if they ignored major mutations in context, failed to recognize significant alterations in the way the image was used?

By the time of *Satura,* Montale's poetry itself seemed to have entered these arguments, taking note of the contradictory interpretations of his "tu," the "you" with which he addresses most of the female figures in his verse, ridiculing biographical and historicist approaches to poetry, looking with a jaundiced eye on attempts to make poetry the function of, or subordinate to, some other system. As the poet's 1975 Nobel Address put it, poetry is "an absolutely useless product."[1] It is likely that Montale here takes a leaf from Crocean aesthetics, which at least in some sense separated practical, utilitarian activity from the pure, disinterested theoretical act. But the poet's praise of a "useless" poetry doubtless represents as well another tribute to his beloved decadent dilettantes, who puttered away at the oddest and most unlikely occupations, never caring to make themselves "useful."

Ultimately, however, these protestations from Montale of poetry's innocence cannot convince. They are defense mechanisms, ferocious ones, and their very existence signifies that the body is infected. From the time of *Ossi di seppia,* Montale's verse is engaged in defensive operations, fighting off the influence of D'Annunzio and his model of the powerful poet whose word is utilitarian in the sense that it is designed to shape and manipulate the public. In short, even *Ossi di seppia* only seems to be innocent of politics, when in fact it has entered the battles of the day by refusing mainstream man (read Fascist man) and his optimism, his confident appropriation of a solid material world. Later hatreds in Montale's poetry for Machine-Age men and for the mob stirred by monstrous credos are thus not abrupt leaps to entirely new topics, but quite comprehensible developments from the starting points of the 1920s.

It has taken a long time to make sense of the politics in Montale's poetry. The late evolutions of his verse have revealed the limitations of those critics who described the poet as a progressive or even a populist writer. But even though the Italian left, at least in its monolithic form, was predictably outraged by the poet's rapid transition from Anti-Fascism to Anti-Communism after the fall of the regime, time will not be too harsh with his judgments on those kinds of states that Hannah Arendt and others have analyzed as totalitarian. Montale was never much of a democrat in the sense of believing in the people, the collectivity, either as subject for art or ultimate source of political authority in a society. But on the other hand his empathy for the Jews, Clizia and others, in the 1930s and 1940s, was hardly the mark of inhuman aloofness. Given that particular mobilization of the many and those particular few, who can maintain that elitism was a vile choice?

Politics has by now come to seem the primal influence on Montale's poetry, overshadowing the metaphysical or existential questions that an earlier generation of critics emphasized. Indeed even in dealing with the literary currents that exerted such force on the poet's development, one can seldom avoid reading a corollary tale of political influence. D'Annunzianism was not a purely literary phenomenon when Montale wrestled with his predecessor in the 1920s, nor was the lesson of the "Twilight" poets, for they were so often deliberate antitheses of D'Annunzio. Then, by the post-World War II era, the interrelationship of literary and political quarrels is plain. Montale's apologies for the decadents intertwine with such political allegories as the story of the Augean stables, while his ideals of an insulated artist and an innocent poetry are unmistakably political polemics.

Conclusion

Have the lyrical poet and the love poet been lost in this insistence on public meanings? Quite to the contrary. For Montale's finest poems of memory, and his most passionate love lyrics can only gain more prestige when one understands that they come from an oeuvre that does not propose mere manipulation of images, sounds, and conventions as its final end.

Notes and References

Chapter One

1. Most of the information in this chapter comes from Giulio Nascimbeni's biography of the poet. Montale was a notoriously reluctant source of data about his life and times. Sketches from his *La farfalla di Dinard* (*The Butterfly of Dinard*), such as the "Racconto d'uno sconosciuto" referred to here, provide a useful, if often whimsical, supplement to the official biography.
2. "Intenzioni: intervista immaginaria," in G. Zampa, ed., *Eugenio Montale: Sulla poesia* (Milan: Mondadori, 1976), 80.
3. See Nascimbeni, 33 and 46–48, for these characters. Compare the story of Rebillo given in *La farfalla di Dinard* under the title "Il successo."
4. G. Ungaretti, *Vita d'un uomo: Tutte le poesie* (Milan: Mondadori, 1969), 25.
5. See Richard Huelsenbeck, "En avant Dada: A History of Dadaism," in R. Motherwell, ed., *The Dada Painters and Poets* (New York: G. Wittenborn, 1951) for a commentary on the avant-garde's reaction to World War I. Consult also Frederic Jameson, *Fables of Aggression: Wyndham Lewis, the Modernist as Fascist* (Berkeley: University of California, 1979), for a recent consideration of the link between the avant-garde and Fascism.
6. *Il fuoco*, rpt. (Milan: Mondadori, 1978). See Michael Ledeen, *The First Duce* (Baltimore: Johns Hopkins, 1977) and Nicola Merola, ed., *D'Annunzio e la poesia di massa* (Bari: Laterza, 1979) for recent accounts of D'Annunzio's political and literary influence.
7. "Stile e tradizione," in *Il Baretti*, 15 January 1925; rpt. in Montale's *Auto da fé* (Milan: Il Saggiatore, 1966), 15–19.
8. Montale's comparison is found in "Cinquant'anni di poesia," an interview with Leone Piccioni published in *L'Approdo letterario*, July-September 1966, 116.
9. For the relationship between D'Annunzio and Montale see P. V. Mengaldo's "Da D'Annunzio a Montale," in *La tradizione del Novecento* (Milan: Feltrinelli, 1975), 13–106.
10. For background on Gobetti, consult Luigi Anderlini and Lelio Basso, eds., *Le riviste di Piero Gobetti* (Milan: Feltrinelli, 1961), and Paolo Spriano, *Gramsci e Gobetti* (Turin: Einaudi, 1977).
11. "L'Italia rinunzia?," in *Auto da fé*, 40–44.

12. For a more detailed account of the relationship between Montale and Croce, see my " 'Botta e risposta I': Decadence Defended," forthcoming in *Italian Quarterly*.

13. "Eugenio Montale: *Ossi di seppia*," in *Leonardo*, November 1925, 250.

14. The link made here between Gozzano and Montale is not casual, since as will become apparent in discussions of *Ossi di seppia*, Montale devises his identity as a poet by distinguishing himself both from D'Annunzio, and from the "Twilight" generation, of which Gozzano was the best-known representative. For "Totò Merùmeni" see *Guido Gozzano: Tutte le poesie* (Milan: Mondadori, 1980), 197.

15. The review is discussed in Nascimbeni's biography, 109–10. An engaging equation between Chaplin as *schlemihl* and Arsenio is presented in Gian Paolo Biasin's *Il vento di Debussy: la poesia di Montale nella cultura del Novecento* (Bologna: Il Mulino, 1985).

16. For Montale's relationship to the woman he calls "Clizia," see Luciano Rebay, "Montale, Clizia e l'America," in *Atti del convegno internazionale: La poesia di Eugenio Montale* (Milan: Librex, 1983), 281–308. The Mosca poems cited are "Ballata scritta in una clinica" and "Il pirla," in TLP, 254–55 and 493 respectively. The dialect word "pirla" means "prick."

17. "Quelli che restano," in *Auto da fé*, 92.

18. "Le reazioni di Montale," in A. Cima and C. Segre, eds., *Eugenio Montale: Profilo di un autore* (Milan: Rizzoli, 1977), 194.

19. This episode is reported in S. Guarnieri's "Con Montale a Firenze," in *Atti del convegno internazionale: La poesia di Eugenio Montale*, 115–32.

20. A prime example of this disillusionment with Montale may be found, as a matter of fact, in Guarnieri's previously mentioned "Con Montale a Firenze."

21. "Piccolo testamento," in TLP, 319–20.

22. "Una nuova cultura," in *Il Politecnico*, 29 September 1945.

23. Letter of 17 July 1946 to G. Contini. See "Lettere di Eugenio Montale," in *Atti del convegno internazionale: La poesia di Eugenio Montale*, 33.

24. "Augurio," in *Auto da fé*, 65–67.

25. "Dopo una fuga," in TLP, 448.

26. "Dialogo," in TLP, 378.

27. "È ancora possibile la poesia?," in Montale's *Sulla poesia* (Milan: Mondadori, 1976), 5–14.

28. "L'alluvione ha sommerso il pack dei mobili. . . ." in TLP, 360.

Chapter Two

1. The deduction is made, for example, by Silvio Ramat, *Montale* (Florence: Vallecchi, 1968), 17.
2. "Cinquant'anni di poesia," interview with Montale by Leone Piccioni, in *L'Approdo letterario*, July-September 1966, 113.
3. "Gozzano trent'anni dopo," in *Sulla poesia*, 62.
4. For D'Annunzio's Nietzscheanism, see his preface to the 1888 novel *Il trionfo della morte*, in vol. 1 of *Prose di romanzi* (Milan: Mondadori, 1959), 652–58. Montale's reaction to this posturing is in "D'Annunzio per tutti," in *Sulla poesia*, 299.
5. Sanguineti's analysis appears in *Tra liberty e crepuscolarismo* (Milan: Mursia, 1961), 55.
6. "Intervista immaginaria," in *Sulla poesia*, 565.
7. The reader will recognize in these pages the influence of Harold Bloom's essays *The Anxiety of Influence* (New York: Oxford, 1973) and *A Map of Misreading* (New York: Oxford, 1975). Especially striking parallels can be indicated between Montale's saga of poetic development and Whitman's; the latter case is examined beginning on page 11 in *A Map of Misreading*.
8. See Laura Caretti's "Un caso di affinità: Eugenio Montale," in her *T. S. Eliot in Italia* (Bari: Adriatica, 1968), 49–80.
9. The first definition is Alfredo Gargiulo's, in his introduction to the 1928 edition of *Ossi di seppia;* rpt. in *Letteratura italiana del Novecento* (Florence: Le Monnier, 1958), 453–57. The second is Pietro Pancrazi's, originally published in 1934; rpt. "Eugenio Montale poeta fisico e metafisico," in *Scrittori d'oggi*, series III (Bari: Laterza, 1946). Montale has used the term "metaphysical," albeit with many qualifications, to describe his poetry. See the 1960 interview, "Dialogo con Montale," in *Sulla poesia*, 581–83.
10. "Montale e *La bufera*," in *Una lunga fedeltà*, 80 and 82.
11. These statements may be found in Emilio Papa, *Fascismo e cultura* (Venice-Padua: Marsilio, 1974), 195 and 190, respectively.
12. Ibid., 137.
13. A more extensive treatment of these disputes is found in my article "What We Are *Not:* Montale's Anti-Fascism Revisited," in *Italica* 60, no. 4 (Winter 1983).
14. "Arsenio," in *Circoli*, November-December 1931, 77–101.
15. "Montale e *La bufera*," in *Una lunga fedeltà*, 84.
16. Sanguineti, *Tra liberty e crepuscolarismo*, 34; "Invernale," in *Guido Gozzano: Tutte le poesie*, 149–50.
17. Giovanni Ansaldo, "La piccola borghesia," in Anderlini and Basso, 552.
18. *Storia d'Europa*, 298–302.

19. F. Camon, "Montale," in his *Il mestiere di poeta* (Milan: Lerici, 1965), 81.

20. Dantesque associations and political meanings of "Incontro" are treated in Angelo Jacomuzzi's article on the poem in *Atti del congresso internazionale: La poesia di Montale*, 149–60.

21. "Sull' 'autobiografismo' di Montale," in *Innovazioni tematiche* etc. (Florence: Olschki, 1976).

22. In *Guido Gozzano: Tutte le poesie*, 160.

23. *Storia d'Italia*, 267.

24. "Guerra agli apolitici" (evidently Gobetti's title), in Anderlini and Basso, 342.

25. "Intervista immaginaria," in *Sulla poesia*, 566.

26. A scene of "shipwreck" also appears in "Flussi," TLP, 103–4.

27. See Pascoli's "Il fanciullino," in *Tutte le prose*, vol. I, *Pensieri di varia umanità* (Milan: Mondadori, 1946), 5–56.

28. *Liriche* (Naples: Ricciardi, 1922).

29. "Camillo Sbarbaro," rpt. in *Sulla poesia*, 189–94. See also Montale's real-life parting of ways with the Ligurian poet, "Ricordo di Sbarbaro," in *Sulla poesia*, 335–37.

30. See "Intervista immaginaria," in *Sulla poesia*, 562–63. Early doubts about the equation of Montale with the Ligurians were expressed by Sergio Solmi; see his 1925 piece, now in Forti, *Per conoscere Montale*, 101.

31. *Auto da fé*, 17.

32. "La signorina Felicita ovvero la Felicità," in *Guido Gozzano: Tutte le poesie*, 178. See Montale's reassessment of his early antipathy for Gozzano in "Intervista immaginaria," in *Sulla poesia*, 561.

33. "Intervista immaginaria," in *Sulla poesia*, 563.

34. "Variazioni," in *Sulla poesia*, 106. It should be added that Montale's distrust of the "fanciullino" in this article reflects the influence of Crocean strictures against "irrational" art. The "child" here epitomizes the poet who privileges music over sense—a dangerous attitude, according to Croce. See Chapter 4 for a complete treatment of the Crocean polemic.

35. "Intervista immaginaria," in *Sulla poesia*, 566.

Chapter Three

1. Umberto Morra, ed., *Per Gobetti: Politica arte cultura a Torino 1918–1926* (Firenze: Vallecchi, 1976), 29.

2. "Intervista immaginaria," in *Sulla poesia*, 566.

3. "Intervista immaginaria," in *Sulla poesia*, 567.

4. Croce's book is *La poesia di Dante* (Bari: Laterza, 1921). Montale's article is "L'estetica e la critica," in *Sulla poesia*, 130.

5. T. S. Eliot, "Hamlet and His Problem," in *The Sacred Wood* (London: Butler and Tanner, 1960), 100. In her *Montale and the Occasions of Poetry* (Princeton: Princeton University Press, 1983), Claire Huffman examines Montale's connection to the "objective correlative" and ends by stressing important differences between the two poets.

6. "Montale, Clizia e l'America," in *Atti del congresso internazionale: La poesia di Montale*, 186–88. Compare Forti's surmise in *Eugenio Montale*, 146.

7. *Guido Gozzano: Tutte le poesie*, 91–97.

8. "Dagli *Ossi* alle *Occasioni*," in *Una lunga fedeltà*, 37–38.

9. This discussion of "Carnevale di Gerti" owes much to G. Cambon's essay "The Descent into Time," in *Eugenio Montale's Poetry*, 34–53.

10. But G. Cambon, *Eugenio Montale's Poetry*, 123–24, connects the words to the "Oriental exoticism" found in several poems of *Le occasioni* and *La bufera* that deal with Jewish characters.

11. For the poet's glosses on "una fede feroce" see Lorenzo Greco, "Eugenio Montale: Commento a se stesso. Parte prima: *Le occasioni*," in *Il Ponte*, 31 October 1975, 1140, and Contini and Bettarini, eds., *Opera in versi*, 902.

12. TLP, 711. Montale in fact took inspiration from the real-life Gerti to create the second part of "Dora Markus": see Contini and Bettarini, eds., *Opera in versi*, 898.

13. See Rebay's "Sull' 'autobiografismo' di Montale," in *Innovazioni tematiche*. . . , 75–76.

14. "Due sciacalli al guinzaglio," in *Sulla poesia*, 84.

15. See G. Cambon on the Dantesque associations of this poem, *Eugenio Montale's Poetry*, 62. Cambon's chapter "The Occasions of Epiphany" and Dante Isella's *Eugenio Montale: "Mottetti"* (Milan: Il Saggiatore, 1980) are the indispensable reading guides for the "Motets." Isella's work includes a particularly fine commentary on the musical qualities of Montale's verse.

16. Alfredo Gargiulo, "Le occasioni," in *Nuova antologia*, April 1940; rpt. in *Letteratura italiana del Novecento* (Florence: Le Monnier, 1958), 633–41.

17. "Due sciacalli al guinzaglio," originally in *Corriere della sera*, 16 February 1950, now rpt. in *Sulla poesia*, 86.

18. "Di Gargiulo su Montale," in *Una lunga fedeltà*, 54–55. Contini makes a joke here: as his and Bettarini's critical edition testifies, he was frequently Montale's reader and interpreter in the 1930s.

19. Luciano Rebay has elaborated this explanation of Clizia's senhal. See, for example, "Sull' 'autobiografismo' di Montale," in *Innovazioni tematiche*. . . .

20. *Metamorphoses*, IV:234–70; "Portami il girasole. . . ," in TLP, 53.
21. Croce, *Storia d'Europa nel secolo decimonono*, 298.
22. The piece, "Della poesia d'oggi," is reprinted in *Sulla poesia*, 557–58.
23. "Il grande rifiuto," in *Auto da fé*, 94.
24. G. Cambon, *Eugenio Montale's Poetry*, 71.
25. See, for example, S. Ramat, *Montale*, 114, or G. Cambon, *Eugenio Montale's Poetry*, 83.
26. Contini and Bettarini, eds., *Opera in versi*, 916.
27. The epigraph from the Spanish poet G. A. Bécquer (1836–70) runs "Sobre el bolcán la flor."
28. "Dagli *Ossi* alle *Occasioni*," in *Una lunga fedeltà*, 19.
29. Contini and Bettarini, eds., *Opera in versi*, 921.
30. "Dagli *Ossi* alle *Occasioni*," in *Una lunga fedeltà*, 44.
31. See Rebay, "Sull' 'autobiografismo' di Montale," in *Innovazioni tematiche*. . . .
32. "Intervista immaginaria," in *Sulla poesia*, 568.
33. See L. Greco, "Eugenio Montale: Commento a se stesso. Parte prima: *Le occasioni*," 1141.
34. An idea discussed by Umberto Carpi in *Montale dopo il fascismo* (Padua: Liviana, 1971), 11.
35. S. Guarnieri, *Condizione della letteratura* (Rome: Riuniti, 1975), 280.
36. This is the suggestion of G. Cambon, *Eugenio Montale* (New York: Columbia University, 1972), 24.
37. Quoted in E. Papa, *Il fascismo e la cultura*, 213.
38. G. Ansaldo, "Servirsi della Chiesa," in Anderlini and Basso, eds., *Le riviste di Aero Gobetti*, 554–57.
39. See U. Carpi, *Il poeta e la politica* (Naples: Liguori, 1978), 311–55, for a powerful and original analysis along these lines.
40. Croce, *Storia d'Europa nel secolo decimonono*, 313.

Chapter Four

1. "Montale e *La bufera*," in *Una lunga fedeltà*, 79.
2. Montale's comments indicate that Clizia is not the only female figure in "Finisterre"; as in the "Motets," the poet mixes various strains of his inspiration. See Contini and Bettarini, *Opera in versi*, 939–41.
3. Compare Montale's comment on this line, Contini and Bettarini, 943–44.
4. Contini and Bettarini, 939. This interpretation is offered in the teeth of Montale's resistance to an explanation of the terms.

5. Oreste Macrì and D'Arco Silvio Avalle are the critics who have contested the meaning of this passage. See Forti, 295, note 30 for a succinct account of the problem.
6. Contini and Bettarini, 939.
7. Ibid., 944.
8. Cima and Segre, 194.
9. Lorenzo Greco, "Eugenio Montale: Commento a se stesso. III: Nella bufera e dopo," 69.
10. Plato's *Symposium*, trans. Walter Hamilton Harmondsworth: Penguin, 1981), 81.
11. See Macrì's "Esegesi del terzo libro di Montale," in *Realtà del simbolo* (Florence: Vallecchi, 1968), 123; also Franco Fortini, *Saggi italiani* (Bari: De Donato, 1974), 144–57.
12. For the decadent treatments of the temptress see Salvatore Guglielmino, *Nell'area del decadentismo* (Bologna: Zanichelli, 1978), 13.
13. *Auto da fé*, 25.
14. *Sulla poesia*, 112.
15. "Risposta a un'inchiesta sull'ermetismo," in *Primato*, 1 June 1940.
16. "Montale e *La bufera*," in *Una lunga fedeltà*, 80 and 83.
17. "Parliamo dell'ermetismo," in *Sulla poesia*, 558–61.
18. See, for example, "L'estetica e la critica," in *Sulla poesia*, 141.
19. "La poesia pura," in *Letture di poeti* (Bari: Laterza, 1950), 265–72.
20. Some of these interpretations may be found in A. Jacomuzzi's "Per un 'omaggio' di Montale 'a Rimbaud,' " in *La poesia di Montale* (Turin: Einaudi, 1978), 92–126. Jacomuzzi's article neglects the controversies on Rimbaud of the 1940s, and also fails to come to grips with the problem of Volpe as a "terrestrial" love.
21. See Baudelaire's *Les Paradis Artificiels* (Paris: Garnier Flammarion, 1966) and Rimbaud's *Illuminations*, a study and translation by Wallace Fowlie (New York: Greenwood, 1969). Baudelaire's and Rimbaud's use of the word "assassin" is referred to in Luciano Anceschi's *Autonomia ed eteronomia dell'arte* (Milan: Garzanti, 1976), 180. Anceschi's work, first published in 1936, is a seminal review, in an anti-Crocean direction, of the decadents. As such it attracts Montale's attention: see "Parliamo dell'ermetismo," in *Sulla poesia*, 559.
22. *Auto da fé*, 25.
23. Croce's assessment of decadent elitism is treated in my Ph.D. thesis, *Montale's Anti-Fascist Poetry from "Ossi di seppia" to the Postwar Years* (Columbia University, 1982), 83–136.
24. *Sulla poesia*, 117.
25. *Montale dopo il fascismo*, 70.

26. "Il nuovo romanticismo," in *Primato*, 15 August 1941.
27. *Auto da fé*, 19.
28. See *The Selected Writings of Salvatore Quasimodo*, ed. and trans. Allen Mandelbaum (New York: Farrar, Straus and Cudahy, 1960), 10.
29. *Letteratura e vita nazionale* (Roma: Riuniti, 1975), 116–17.
30. TLP, 714.
31. "Intervista immaginaria," in *Sulla poesia*, 568.
32. Ibid.
33. Carpi, *Montale dopo il fascismo*, 117–21.
34. Thus "L'Italia rinunzia" (1945), in *Auto da fé*, 40–44, insists that Gobetti was a "bourgeois hero," implies that the intelligentsia was the most significant anti-Fascist force, and claims that the masses of Italian people cannot be expected to govern themselves.
35. Carpi, *Montale dopo il fascismo*, 67.
36. "La 'Lettera a Malvolio,' " in Cima and Segre, 153.

Chapter Five

1. Annalisa Cima, ed., "Le reazioni di Montale," in Cima and Segre, eds., *Eugenio Montale*, 196.
2. "L'estetica e la critica," in *Sulla poesia*, 129.
3. "Il Decadentismo," in A. Momigliano, ed., *Questioni e correnti di storia letteraria*, vol. II, *Problemi ed orientamenti critici di lingua e di letteratura italiana* (Milan: Marzorati, 1949), 775.
4. "Il fascismo e la letteratura," in *Auto da fé*, 23.
5. See "Esiste un 'decadentismo' in Italia?," in *Sulla poesia*, 113, and "Gobetti," in the *Corriere della sera*, 16 February 1951.
6. "Esiste un 'decadentismo' in Italia?," in *Sulla poesia*, 116.
7. "Montale e *La bufera*," in *Una lunga fedeltà*, 92.
8. See Maria Corti, "*Satura* e il genere 'diario poetico,' " rpt. in Marco Forti, ed., *Per conoscere Montale*, 291.
9. Montale makes this point, for example, in "Parliamo dell'ermetismo," in *Sulla poesia*, 559.
10. The Mosca poems are identified by Montale in Lorenzo Greco's "Eugenio Montale: Commento a se stesso. IV. *Satura*," in *Il Ponte*, 31 October 1977, 1198.
11. *Ibid.*, 1195.
12. "L'estetica e la critica," in *Sulla poesia*, 142.
13. Ibid., 565.
14. P. P. Pasolini, "*Satura*," in *Nuovi argomenti*, January-March, 1971, 17–20.
15. See the account of this exchange in Enzo Siciliano, *Pasolini: A Biography*, trans. John Shepley (New York: Random House, 1982), 352–56.

16. Annalisa Cima, ed., "Le reazioni di Montale," in Cima and Segre, eds., *Eugenio Montale*, 192.

17. Compare Montale's early predilection for marginal spaces, as discussed by Rebecca West, *Eugenio Montale* (Cambridge: Harvard University, 1982), 11–38.

18. I translate from the Italian given in Contini and Bettarini, eds., *Opera in versi*, 1035. Luciano Rebay's English translation may be found in the *American Scholar*, 40, no. 3 (Summer 1971):416–20.

19. Contini and Bettarini, eds., *Opera in versi*, 694. The poem, "Ho tanta fede in te. . . ." ("I have such great faith in you. . . ."), like others mentioned in this section, is from *Altri versi*. (The exception is "Annetta," which appears in *Diario del '72*.)

20. Annalisa Cima, ed., "Le reazioni di Montale," in Cima and Segre, eds., *Eugenio Montale*, 195.

Chapter Six

1. "È ancora possibile la poesia?," in *Sulla poesia*, 6.

Selected Bibliography

PRIMARY SOURCES

1. Collections

Altri versi. Milan: Mondadori, 1981.
Auto da fé: Cronache in due tempi. Milan: Il Saggiatore, 1966.
Eugenio Montale: L'opera in versi. Edited by Gianfranco Contini and Rosanna Bettarini. Turin: Einaudi, 1980.
Eugenio Montale: Sulla poesia. Edited by Giorgio Zampa. Milan: Mondadori, 1976.
Farfalla di Dinard. Milan: Mondadori, 1969.
Quaderno di traduzioni. Milan: Mondadori, 1975.
Tutte le poesie. Milan: Mondadori, 1977.

2. English Translations

Arrowsmith, William, trans. and ed. *The Storm and Other Things.* New York and London: W. W. Norton, 1985.
Cambon, Glauco, introd. *Eugenio Montale: Selected Poems.* New York: New Directions, 1965.
Farnsworth, Edith, trans. *Provisional Conclusions: A Selection of the Poetry of Eugenio Montale.* Chicago: Henry Regnery Co., 1970.
Galassi, Jonathan, trans. *Eugenio Montale: Selected Essays.* New York: Ecco Press, 1983.
Kay, George, trans. *Selected Poems of Eugenio Montale.* Baltimore: Penguin, 1969.
Singh, Ghanshyam, trans. *The Butterfly of Dinard.* Lexington: University of Kentucky, 1971.
———. *Eugenio Montale: New Poems.* New York: New Directions, 1976.
———. *Eugenio Montale: Selected Essays.* Manchester: Carcanet, 1978.
———, trans. and introd. *It Depends: A Poet's Notebook.* New York: New Directions, 1980.
Wright, Charles, trans. *The Storm and Other Poems.* Oberlin: Field Translation Series, 1978.

SECONDARY SOURCES

Almansi, Guido, and **Bruce Merry.** *Eugenio Montale: The Private Language of Poetry.* Edinburgh: Edinburgh University, 1977. Eclectic forays into source study and formal analysis; a complete reading of the poet's verse is attempted.

Atti del convegno internazionale: La poesia di Eugenio Montale. Milano-Genova, 12–15 September 1982. (Milan: Librex, 1983). Includes essays by Silvio Guarnieri on Montale's Anti-Fascism, Luciano Rebay on Clizia, and Oreste Macrì on Montale's poetics, among others.

Avalle, D'Arco Silvio. *Tre saggi su Montale.* Turino: Einaudi, 1972. Thematic studies, including an analysis of "angelic" imagery.

Barile, Laura, ed. *Bibliografia montaliana.* Milan: Mondadori, 1977. Lists more than two thousand works by Montale.

Becker, Jared. "What We Are Not: Montale's Anti-Fascism Revisited." *Italica,* Winter 1983. Metaphysics and politics in *Ossi di seppia.*

Cambon, Glauco. *Eugenio Montale's Poetry: A Dream in Reason's Presence.* Princeton: Princeton University, 1982. A collection of essays, including chapters on the "Motets" and Dantesque influences in Montale.

Carpi, Umberto. *Montale dopo il fascismo dalla 'Bufera' a 'Satura.'* Padua: Liviana, 1971. A key political exegesis of Montale, with emphasis on the postwar period.

——. *Il poeta e la politica: Belli, Leopardi, Montale.* Naples: Liguori, 1978. Contains a discussion of Montale's elitism, and analyzes "Elegia di Pico Farnese."

Cima, Annalisa, and Cesare Segre, eds. *Profilo di un autore: Eugenio Montale.* Milan: Rizzoli, 1977. Contains essays by Andrea Zanzotto on "Botta e risposta I" and Pier Vincenzo Mengaldo on "Lettera a Malvolio."

Contini, Gianfranco. *Una lunga fedeltà: Scritti su Eugenio Montale.* Turin: Einaudi, 1974. Still the most authoritative guide to many aspects of the early Montale. Political questions receive only passing attention.

Forti, Marco. *Eugenio Montale: La poesia, la prosa di fantasia e d'invenzione.* Milan: Mursia, 1974. The most comprehensive line-by-line commentary on the poet's work.

——, ed. *Per conoscere Montale.* Milan: Mondadori, 1976. Contains an extensive bibliography, and reprints essays by Sergio Solmi on *Ossi di seppia* and Maria Corti on *Satura,* among others.

Huffman, Claire de C. L. *Montale and the Occasions of Poetry.* Princeton: Princeton University Press, 1983. Essays on *Le occasioni* and *La bufera.*

Jacomuzzi, Angelo. *La poesia di Montale: Dagli 'Ossi' ai 'Diari.'* Turin: Einaudi, 1978. Close readings of several poems, including "Botta e risposta I," and an insistence on Montale's verse as allegorical.

Letture montaliane in occasione dell'ottantesimo compleanno del Poeta. Genoa: Bozzi Editore, 1978. The collection includes essays by Cesare Goffis on "Arsenio," Laura Barile on "Crisalide," Riccardo Scrivano on "La storia," as well as pieces by Italo Calvino and Leonardo Sciascia.

Lonardi, Gilberto. *Il vecchio e il giovane.* Bologna: Zanichelli, 1980. Connections between Montale and Browning, Leopardi, Foscolo, and Shakespeare.

Luperini, Romano. *Montale o l'identità negata.* Naples: Liguori, 1984. Excellent observations on Montale's politics, on the fading of Clizia in *La bufera,* and on such themes as the dead and the modern metropolis in the poet's work.

Macrì, Oreste. *Realtà del simbolo.* Florence: Vallecchi, 1968. Contains an exegesis of *La bufera e altro.*

Mengaldo, Pier Vincenzo. *La tradizione del Novecento.* Milan: Feltrinelli, 1975. Includes an exacting study of the literary relationship between D'Annunzio and Montale.

Nascimbeni, Giulio. *Eugenio Montale.* Milan: Longanesi, 1975. The official biography. Gives details about the poet's Ligurian years and tenure at the *Corriere della sera.* Makes use of the poet's semiautobiographical writings.

La poesia di Eugenio Montale: Atti del Convegno Internazionale tenuto a Genova, 1982. Florence: Le Monnier, 1984. Essays on the poet's "obscurity," on "Botta e risposta," and on early critical reaction to Montale.

Ramat, Silvio, ed. *Omaggio a Montale.* Milan: Mondadori, 1966. The homage includes extracts from fifty years of critical works on Montale.

Rebay, Luciano. "Sull' 'autobiografismo' di Montale." In *Innovazioni tematiche espressive e linguistiche della letteratura italiana del Novecento.* Atti dell'VIII congresso dell'Assn. internazionale per gli studi di lingua e letteratura italiana, New York, 25–28 aprile 1973. Florence: Olschki, 1976. Information on the Arletta cycle.

Singh, Ghanshyam. *Eugenio Montale: A Critical Study of His Poetry, Prose, and Criticism.* New Haven: Yale University, 1973. A methodical commentary with extensive quotation and translation.

West, Rebecca. *Eugenio Montale: Poet on the Edge.* Cambridge: Harvard University, 1981. Thematic and linguistic studies of Montale's verse.

Index

Arendt, Hannah, 116, 138
Arletta (Annetta), 13, 18, 42–44, 72–76, 81, 94–96, 114, 127, 132, 135–36
Arsenio, 33–36, 64–65, 118, 120–21
Auden, W. H., 17

Baudelaire, Charles, 5
Beardsley, Aubrey, 100
Bergson, Henri, 2
Boccaccio, 17
Bottai, Giuseppe, 13
Browning, Robert, 52, 117

Cambon, Glauco, 59, 69
Campana, Dino, 127
Carducci, Giosuè, 4, 21, 50
Carpi, Umberto, 106, 113, 115
Ceva, Tommaso, 102
Cervantes, 2, 13, 75, 77
Chaplin, Charles, 10–11
Chardin, Teilhard de, 17, 130
Chrysalis-woman (Crisalide), 38–42, 45–46
Clizia (Irma Brandeis), 11–14, 16, 18, 41, 47, 55, 61–62, 64–65, 67–72, 78–88, 91, 96–99, 108–14, 119, 127–28, 132, 133, 135–36
Constantine, King of Greece, 123
Contini, Gianfranco, 14, 30, 36, 57, 64, 77, 86, 101, 108, 121
Corazzini, Sergio, 49
Croce, Benedetto, 2, 6, 8–10, 15–16, 31, 33, 38, 44, 53, 68, 82–83, 85, 100, 102–3, 116, 117, 120, 123, 128–29, 137

D'Annunzio, Gabriele, 4–6, 17, 18, 21, 25, 33, 38–39, 44, 49–50, 75, 100, 102, 122, 129, 137–38
Dante, 6, 17, 39–40, 42, 45, 53, 62–63, 70
Debussy, Claude, 1
Decadence, 100–106, 117–22, 128–29
Dostoevski, Fedor, 10
Du Bellay, Joachim, 19

Einaudi, Luigi, 6

Eliot, T. S., 16, 28, 34, 35, 53, 101
Esterina, 36–38, 44

Fadin, Sergio, 95
Farinacci, Roberto, 52
Faulkner, William, 13
Flora, Francesco, 118
Fox-woman (Volpe), 16, 47, 86, 96–100, 113, 127–28, 132
France, Anatole, 100

Gandhi, Mahatma, 16
Gargiulo, Alfredo, 9, 63–64
Gerti, 58–59, 119
Gide, André, 17
Gobetti, Piero, 6–8, 31–32, 33, 37–38, 45, 83
Gozzano, Guido, 10, 17, 37, 44, 50, 57, 75
Gramsci, Antonio, 83, 108, 120
Guarnieri, Silvio, 81

Hawthorne, Nathaniel, 13
Hemingway, Ernest, 17
Hermeticism, 101–2, 131
Hitler, Adolf, 93, 111–12
Hopkins, Gerard Manley, 101
Hugo, Victor, 5
Huysmans, J. K., 100

Joyce, James, 7

Kafka, Franz, 17
Keats, John, 2

Leopardi, Giacomo, 10, 17, 77
Levi, Carlo, 10, 83
Liuba, 11, 14, 58–60, 69, 86, 110, 119

Marcì, Oreste, 100
Mallarmé, Stéphane, 103
Mann, Thomas, 15
Markus, Dora, 11, 14, 58–61, 83, 86, 110
Melville, Herman, 13
Mengaldo, P. V., 116
Mosca (Drusilla Tanzi), 12, 18, 93, 124–29, 132, 137
Mussolini, Benito, 6, 10, 30, 33, 86, 92, 111–12, 120, 131

Nestorian, The, 99, 110–11, 130

Pascoli, Giovanni, 4, 6, 17, 21, 49, 50–51
Pasolini, Pier Paolo, 17, 83, 130–31
Pavese, Casare, 10, 83
Petrini, Domenico, 45
Pintor, Giaime, 14, 107
Pirandello, Luigi, 102
Plato, 98
Pound, Ezra, 16, 127
Pratolini, Vasco, 31
Prezzolini, Giuseppe, 6, 9, 45
Proust, Marcel, 7

Quasimodo, Salvatore, 107, 109

Rebay, Luciano, 44, 78
Rimbaud, Arthur, 9, 16, 101, 103–4
Sanguineti, Edoardo, 25–26, 37
Sartre, Jean Paul, 17
Sbarbaro, Camillo, 47–48, 49, 100
Shakespeare, 70

Sivori, Ernesto, 1–2, 57
Snow, C. P., 68
Solmi, Sergio, 3
Stalin, Joseph, 115
Stein, Gerturde, 125
Steinbeck, John, 13
Svevo, Italo, 7, 108

Theresa of Avila, 75
Twain, Mark, 13
Twilight poets, 25–26, 49, 64–65, 75

Ungaretti, Giuseppe, 3, 101–3, 125

Valéry, Paul, 7, 101, 103, 127
Verlaine, Paul, 26
Visconti, Luchino, 83
Vittorini, Elio, 13, 15, 35–36, 107–8

Wilde, Oscar, 100

THE LIBRARY
ST. MARY'S COLLEGE OF MARYLAND
ST. MARY'S CITY, MARYLAND 20686